STONEY BALONEY

BY ALEX RUSSON

FOREWORD

This is the story of a golfing friendship that turns sour. It's been a painful journey so I've thrown in some sporadic memories of Stonehaven to lighten the atmosphere.

Thank you to those who assisted in the production of this book –

Ian Hastie, Ian Wood, Karen Murray, Terry Wilson, Bryan Innes, Andrew Locke, Chris Taylor, Grant Robb, Carolyn Duncan, Catherine MacDonald, Joe Riddell, Karen Smith, Ian Smith, Graham Garden.

Stoney Baloney has a Facebook page

Third hole

CHAPTER ONE

'Metropolis, has nothing on this'
Depeche Mode

Stonehaven Golf Club has spent over a century clinging to the coastline a mile north of the town, providing spectacular views and a test of golf. It's a green blanket perched precariously above the cliffs, sloping from left to right, peering down upon the North Sea below. Along with the War Memorial, which sits equidistantly to the south of the town, the golf club majestically bookends Stonehaven.

For the uninitiated, and the disingenuous, it would appear golf could not be played on such lopsided terrain. From a distance, the slopes appear so severe that members might require a portable platform from which to secure an even stance, sheep should be grazing or crops grown, not golf played. In truth, however, only five holes (3rd, 5th, 10th, 13th and 17th) genuinely yield an uncomfortable second shot stance, provided you're playing anything approaching sensible golf, and every other shot should afford a level playing field. Stonehaven's golf course isn't appreciated on the north of Scotland circuit as well as it might be, mocked by snooty golfers demanding stereotypical links golf with Open championship romance. Stonehaven has idiosyncratic slopes which deters certain golfers who flounce off to Montrose, Royal Aberdeen, Murcar and the like, instead. That's fair enough, you pay your money and you take your choice, but for the members of Stonehaven, and there are six hundred of us, the club is our second home, a sanctuary, it's dear to us. I won't attempt to defend it, it doesn't need defending.

Some describe it as a 'Marmite' golf course, love it or hate it, if so, I know at least five hundred and ninety nine people who adore Marmite. And while many golfing visitors to the north east of Scotland frequent the rolling fairways of alternative courses, we members at Stonehaven happily nestle on the cliffside, pushing our trolleys and carrying our bags around a piece of land offering awe inspiring views, smooth greens and a warm kinship. It's a special place.

I was 12 years old when I first started playing golf at Stoney, alongside a dozen or so lads who were as fanatical as I was, we virtually lived up there. We'd play in all weathers, at all times, unless the tee was reserved for adult members (the majority of whom we could beat without breaking sweat). We understood the rules and conventions of the club though, we knew our place and gained the respect of senior members with this attitude. Gordon Locke and Clive Lloyd ran the Junior section and instilled in us an understanding of golf's etiquette, consequently members treated us respectfully in return. Not that many of these members took pity on us when passing in their cars on the road up to the club mind, bloody long walk that, a lift would have been appreciated.

Whatever the weather, we were up at the club, wrapped up like eskimos in the cold, bedecked in waterproofs in the wet and turning a shade of crimson in the heat. The six week summer holidays were devoted to berry picking for one week and golf for five, our parents barely saw us. The routine was to cycle up to the golf club for 9am, play eighteen holes, sit by the clubhouse window with a plate of pie and beans then haul yourself out for eighteen more. Occasionally we'd sneak in another ten holes with the adults after they'd finished work, or goof around on the practice green competing in endless putting contests. We were all about golf, golf and more golf. We'd sleep, we'd eat and we'd play golf. If the weather meant we couldn't get onto the course we'd play snooker or three card brag in the clubhouse until it cleared up. Playing golf did so much for our lives, it taught us about rules, behaviours, patience, tolerance, and competition. The miles we walked were good for our health and most of us reached a good standard, sufficient to equip us with a sporting capability to last the rest of our lives.

My Dad was a member but rarely played through the week, he wouldn't return from work in time unless it was midsummer. He played most Saturdays though, usually in a fourball permed from Eric Soutar, Eric Douglas, Francis Hart and Roy Kane. Eric Soutar was my Mum's Uncle and a larger than life figure, my family association with him gave me a certain swagger. Mid-fifties, droopy ginger moustache, a diamond Pringle sweater and distinctive walk since one leg was shorter than the other. If you didn't see him coming you'd certainly hear him, a loud booming voice, diabolical language and a piercing cackle. He wasn't everyone's cup of tea, certainly not the committee's, he treated the course like his own private practice area, larruping irons from the third tee to the practice green or pitching half a dozen balls onto the second green in full glare of the clubhouse. He'd never play the gruelling gully holes, unless involved in a competition, and instead played the first four holes of the course before hopping onto the field (9-12) to play it twice before finishing with the sixteenth and seventeenth. I caddied for him once in the club championship only to find myself fetching his putter from the railway track after he'd three putted for par after driving the green. Eric loved Jack Nicklaus and it was my pleasure to follow

7

Nicklaus around St Andrews during a British Open practice day in 1984 and obtain his autograph. I proudly handed it to Eric but he didn't believe it was genuine, it was later inherited by his grandson Alexs. It's pucker Alexs I promise you.

All of that was back in the eighties but at the age of forty six, after a thirty year break from living in Stonehaven, I returned to the area. I'd spent the intervening three decades back in Birmingham, my family had relocated from there when I was twelve. This time round though it was my turn to relocate a family, I came with a wife and three children, to live in Auchenblae, which sits inland, ten miles south of Stonehaven.

My new neighbour, Ally, invited me for a game at Edzell Golf Club where he'd been a member for over twenty years. Edzell sits a further ten miles south of Auchenblae and its golf course is beautiful, long and challenging. I played like a drain (tellingly he hasn't invited me back) but I appreciated the opportunity to learn more about my new neighbour, the village of Auchenblae and to experience a new golf course. We retired to the bar afterwards where Ally explained the joining procedure were I to apply. I'd enjoyed the course and quite liked the idea of regular golf with my likeable new neighbour, membership was a serious consideration. The following week however, Jack Douglas, a good friend of mine who'd remained in touch throughout my thirty year absence from the area, invited me with his son, Connor, and brother, Keith, to play in an annual Fourball competition at Stonehaven. I fell right back in love with the place the moment I pulled into the car park. I was thrilled to be striding the fairways again, somewhat choked, I don't mind telling you, at being back at my spiritual home. Any prospect of me applying for Edzell membership evaporated there and then.

Rose tinted spectacles? Perhaps, but while the head told me to choose Edzell for its golfing challenge, the heart overruled. One particular memory came to mind as I played Stonehaven that weekend, a recollection of horrendous playing conditions which I'd endured one late afternoon as a teenager. I remembered being on the second tee, alone beneath leaden skies, dark clouds blackening by the second, thunder bellowing and rain spitting gradually until soaking me with a deluge of biblical proportions. I remember feeling so alive, an otherwise unimpressionable teenager revelling in a moment that nature had inspired, and rather than sprinting to the clubhouse to seek cover, I'd absorbed the drama of the moment, exposed against the brutal elements but loving every second, rain hammering down, wind blowing a gale, thunder crashing around me, it was thrilling. Yet, within minutes the rain had subsided, the sky brightened and a perfect rainbow formed over the North Sea, a breath taking few moments I'd remembered to this day. This is why I would join Stonehaven in favour of Edzell. Dramatic scenery, happy memories but most of all, a giant tug on the heart strings.

Upon completion of my fourball with the Douglas clan, I returned to the clubhouse and asked what the damage would be were a new member to join.

'£100 winter membership, £495 full membership next year and your £100 winter fee knocked off if you convert to full membership' said Joe. 'No joining fee either.'

'No joining fee? I should hope not. I demand appearance money, I'm a former junior champion.'

'You can ask for appearance money by all means sir,' he replied politely, 'but I wouldn't hold out hope of a positive outcome. Anyhow, who says you were a junior champion?'

I drew myself to my full height and suggested he take a peek at the Junior Championship scroll of honour over by the snooker table where he would find incontrovertible proof. Back in 1986, when I was sixteen years of age, I'd achieved what was to become the pinnacle of my golfing career, winning the Stonehaven Golf Club Junior Championship. I won it following an eighteen hole play off after tying with Frank McCarron and leaving Bryan Innes (future Scotland international) and David Ross (future Royal Aberdeen professional) trailing in my wake. You're no doubt familiar with this already, my place assured alongside the other greats of the game; Woods, Ballesteros, Norman, Faldo, Russon... the names roll off the tongue.

Back to today though and the winter membership offer was tempting. Winters on the east coast can be gruelling but I'd sooner be cold on a golf course than cosy in a warm house, pleading with my children to tidy their rooms and carrying out household chores. I was in, and with the winter league due to commence within a fortnight, I committed to entering the doubles competition in an attempt to familiarise myself with a few of the members. I just needed a partner. Keith Douglas was stood next to me, a man not usually renowned for leaving his scratcher to play golf in the winter months, but he offered to partner me and I accepted. My rebirth at Stonehaven Golf Club would start here.

I wasn't sure how this partnership would unfold. Keith and I played hours of golf together back in the 80s but weren't good for each other's game, we didn't take our golf seriously enough and spent more time winding each other up than striving for golfing excellence. We'd snigger at each other's misfortune

10

rather than sympathise, mercilessly needle one another and had an unfortunate common ailment; that of overt flatulence. We'd be breaking wind from the first tee to the last green and in a memorable round of golf in sweltering heat at Royal Hoylake with Keith's brother Jack, completed a dishonourable draw of forty two guffs apiece while accompanying Jack to a creditable round of two over par. Nevertheless, with Keith now pleading with me to accompany him, we duly entered the winter league 2016, committing to a weekly game for three months, our best ten best scores counting towards an aggregate which would determine whether we qualified for the grand final in March.

CHAPTER TWO

'I'm hoping I don't freeze here'
Badly Drawn Boy

Round 1 – October 17th 2015

A dry, breezy morning and a dozen or so irritable golfers wait to strike their first blows in the Stonehaven Golf Club Winter League. They're being held up by slow play and shoddy time keeping, the early players had turned up late causing a domino effect of delay and with the new winter tee offering the chance to drive the first green, they've had to wait for it to clear before teeing off.

Summer tees were now rested to protect them from the rigours of winter so the dreaded mats were to be our launch pads for the next few months, the first one situated directly beneath the clubhouse, your backswing practically reaching the optics behind the bar. Other changes in the winter golf rule book included removing your ball from the fairway to play from the nearest semi rough instead, a blessing really since you could place your ball upon a fluffy tuft of turf, beautiful, particularly if you've just removed your ball from a fairway divot.

There was a hell of a stink in front of the clubhouse, we were teeing off with pegs on our noses. The gents toilets had become blocked and the build up of decaying matter, the morning after a Friday night's excess, gave off an odour that fair brought tears to the eyes. Brenda behind the bar had been informed of the lavatory malfunction so scrawled OUT OF ORDER on a piece of A4 and asked Willie Donald to do something with it.

'Fit d'ya want me to dee wi' it like?' asked Willie.

'Stick it on your forehead' I quipped, feeling very pleased with myself. Willie didn't smile, I left the vicinity, tumbleweed swept in.

Keith had announced upon my arrival that he would birdie the first, a pleasing habit he often executed following a break from the game, and blow me if he didn't do just that. A booming drive, a flick to five feet and a tram lined putt into the centre. When he followed it with another three on the second I congratulated myself on a good choice of winter league partner. It took me until the seventh to contribute anything of note during which time the temperature, typical of Stonehaven, had lurched from cool to Baltic to warm. I started the round dressed in two layers, increased to three and was down to shirt sleeves (and trousers) by the seventh. Welcome back to golf in the north east of Scotland.

A steady performance from Keith carried us to a creditable opening score of 67 with my contribution best described as fitful. Only on three holes did my score improve upon his which was rather humbling, Noteworthy occurrences –

* Asking the fourball in front of us to get a shift on when they fell two holes behind those in front of them. A terse reply was chuntered however my admonishment had the desired effect. They were a bit frosty in the clubhouse afterwards, miffed that a brand new member was telling them to sort themselves out, but hey ho, someone had to tell 'em.

* My tee shot on the last hole was flying towards oblivion until crashing off the cemetery wall and rebounding to six feet. Typical of my limp performance, I failed to take

advantage, giving my birdie attempt no hope at all before sheepishly nudging in for a par.

- I slid my hand into a rarely visited golf bag pocket, in search of a pencil, only to discover a liquidised mouldy apple. I estimate it had sat there fermenting for twelve months.

- The winter league scoring system was explained to me several times during the round and I was none the wiser by the finish. It would require more than an abacus to sort this out when the final scores were totted up in March.

- I texted my wife Kate afterwards to say I was running late, her reply required me to buy nail varnish remover and oven chips on my way home. I mention this purely for its random nature.

Our next round will be in a fortnight. We should be participating next week but Keith's in Germany visiting the Becks beer factory (no I'm not joking).

*   *   *

As an aside, today was my tenth wedding anniversary and the theme for the tenth year is tin. I therefore wrapped Kate's card in bacofoil, but failed to explain my actions which caused much confusion. Realising she hadn't clocked quite why I'd wrap something up in kitchen foil, I let it ride, leaving her to scratch her head like they do in the sitcoms. I wasn't meant to buy her a gift but disregarded our convention in an attempt to impress. Instead she was horrified that she'd bought me nothing so within twenty four hours I was the proud owner of Steve Coogan's autobiography, thereby striking another idea off the Christmas list. We dined at The Creel Inn, Catterline, a small fish restaurant come boozer. A table candle lent a little romance to the occasion, a blessing since I'm incapable of so doing. I'd bought flowers earlier in the day and a pot plant since I couldn't choose between the two (flowers have a short life, plants are longer lasting which appealed to my sense of prudency). For once, we managed to converse about topics other than our children and the unavailability of wifi meant Kate couldn't be rescued by her i-phone, there was no escape for the poor woman. We shared memories of our wedding day and looked at the photo album when we returned home, it was peculiar to see so many people who we're barely in touch with anymore, Lee Cathcart was amongst them, prompting memories of many footballing escapades when he and I were members of St Marys FC. I loved playing football with Lee, he was the only player in the squad that made me look good.

CHAPTER THREE

'The most inept that ever stepped'
The Smiths

Round 2 October 31st 2015

Nothing takes the wind out of an expectant golfer's sails like a 'Course Closed' sign as he pulls into the car park. Heavy rainfall had waterlogged the course sufficiently for the greenkeeper to send the early starters from whence they came, the place was deserted by 10am. Nonetheless, Keith and I shared a couple of frames of snooker in the clubhouse hoping that the course might re-open if we waited long enough, an hour later our patience was rewarded. No further rain, course open, green grass replacing green baize (thank goodness, I thought my golf was bad but hells bells, I couldn't pot a plant never mind a red).

Two other guys, Craig and Graham, made up the fourball. I assumed Keith knew them since they kept calling him 'Sheepo', not something you'd ordinarily address a stranger as. _(Mental note : ask Keith why the hell people nickname him Sheepo)._

I had a quiet word with myself before play began. Keith had owned up to being a somewhat reluctant winter league player since his chivalrous invite to partner me and the prospect of rising from his pit early on a Saturday morning wasn't appetising to him. I needed to devise a way of maintaining his enthusiasm, ensure his sustained interest, find a way to keep him in the habit of golfing on a Saturday throughout the cold winter months to come. So I hatched a plan.

In the first round I felt I'd been rather greedy with my share in our combined betterball score of 67. I'd notched three contributions out of the eighteen holes which, while at first sight, may appear paltry, was in fact a stellar performance given I was suffering with a blocked up nose . So I decided to step back a little this week, fall on my sword, allow Keith rather more prominence, a more significant slice of the pie. If his score was such that he could walk away feeling puffed up with his importance, proud and invigorated, it would encourage him to come back again next week rather than sink deeper under the covers to nurse the after effects of a Friday night Stoney bender.

I therefore proceeded to contribute precisely nothing to this week's score, quite literally not improving upon Keith's tally on one single hole. Some might suggest this to be overly generous, perhaps bordering on the insulting that I should be so overtly full of grace and goodwill. Let me say to such accusers that I understand your standpoint. Why would someone be so giving in nature as to afford his partner all of the credit when in truth the two of them were participating in a team game? My response to that assertion is simple however; what kind of world would this be if a little benevolence wasn't evidenced every once in a while? Our planet is dominated by the selfish and the egotistical, celebrities are fawned over and notoriety appears to be the only ambition of our youth today. It's vital, I feel, that the brotherhood of man progresses from its single minded, self-centredness and instead encourages the fellow man to share the limelight once in a while. We must surely, in all humility, give a little. In my own small way, therefore, I poured a little of the milk of human kindness upon Keith by allowing him to score a singlehanded 63 with no assistance from myself whatsoever. He made four birdies, thirteen pars and countless clutch putts, but I'd like to think he sat before an open fire on Saturday evening, resplendent in his smoking jacket, swirling his brandy around the rim of a crystal glass, humbly raising a toast to a winter league golfing partner who had the humility to step aside and allow him his moment in the sun. All I can say is that it was my pleasure Keith and I haven't ruled out repeating it (week after week after week).

CHAPTER FOUR

'There are places I'll remember, all my life,
though some have changed'
The Beatles

Back in 1982, when I was informed I'd be attending Mackie Academy following my family's relocation from Birmingham, I assumed my parents had found an elite school to harness the extraordinary talent they'd spotted in me. You don't get 'academies' in England, just secondary schools, I attended Arthur Terry Secondary School in Sutton Coldfield for example. I was soon to discover though that academies were merely equivalents of secondary schools so put my halo back in the cupboard.

Mr Fraser was the Rector, another diversion for me, I was accustomed to headmasters leading schools, not rectors. He wore a flowing black gown which threw me at first viewing but there weren't many viewings after that apart from the occasional assembly. The school had a good reputation which had attracted my parents to Stonehaven rather than Aberdeen, along with the house prices. It was attended by the town's children and those of various neighbouring villages including Portlethen and Newtonhill to the north, Johnshaven and Inverbervie to the south. At this time, early eighties, Portlethen wasn't quite the sprawling mass of people that it is today and didn't have its own school (or golf club for that matter). It was still however the largest feeder of children to Mackie Academy beyond residents of Stonehaven itself, and as a newcomer I could see a very definite difference in the kids that travelled in from the north of Stoney and the kids from the south. I'll try and be delicate here without offending either camp, while probably offending both, but let's just say that those students from the Portlethen district were more akin to the inner city Birmingham kids I'd grown up with in terms of their approach to schooling. Those from the southern, coastal villages were of a different nature, speaking a language that appeared to be from another planet and having little to do with those not from their villages, they were from the farming community and appeared to have a language all of their own, not easy when you're a Brummy kid, tattie picking for the first time while trying to follow instructions without getting yer airse skelped.

Mackie boasted around a thousand students at this time and my house tutor/registration teacher/can't remember his proper title, was Mr Jaffray. I was in Dunnottar house, the red one, and my class was DB1. Mr Jaffray was great, very matter of fact and critically to a schoolkid, not at all strict, he had a laissez fare attitude. You wouldn't want to take advantage of his relaxed approach but you'd certainly push the boundaries. My first impressions were of a welcoming school, with approachable teachers who were accommodating towards this nervous, frightened twelve year old from Birmingham, apart from one teacher who used me as a target when unloading his nationalistic tendencies, but it was no big deal. I had a massive hang up over accents, I'd convinced myself before moving up that I wouldn't understand a blind word anyone was saying and they wouldn't understand me, so it was a relief to discover we understood each other fully apart from the odd problem with dialect (eg. They hadn't a clue if I said 'bostin' and I was dumbfounded when asked 'fit like min'?). Teachers tried to help me acclimatise to my new surroundings and because I wasn't giving it the large one, the kids took to me. Some were intrigued by my accent and my background, most couldn't give a stuff and simply accepted me as they would anyone else. My jotters were always covered in AVFC daubings, Villa became my identity I suppose, they were big news back then having just won the league and about to win the European Cup, so there was a grudging respect of the football team I supported. English football hooliganism was at its height (depth?) so I'd be probed about English football 'firms' too, I knew nothing about them but didn't let on.

I settled in fine at Mackie, just as my brothers Stu and Chris did at Dunnottar Primary. I established friendships and performed adequately in my studies, never top set, never bottom, just coasting along somewhere in the middle, doing enough to get by while never pushing myself beyond minimum requirements. Teachers get wise to students who want to excel and those who want to get by, they soon bracketed me accordingly. English, History, Maths and Modern Studies I was good at, any science or technical subject though was a complete no-no so I grubbed along, scraping through exams by the skin of my teeth. Like father like son, my abilities in any subject of a technical nature were somewhere between crap and pathetic although I did become the talk of the school when it came to a particular Woodwork lesson. Mr Christie showed us a video about accidents in the workshop and it made me feel queasy. I left the room in search of the toilet and after staggering a few yards up the corridor, fainted, landing in a heap right outside the opened door of a classroom of younger kids who found it hilarious. I was carted off to the school nurse after I'd come round thirty seconds later, bleeding from the head and being mocked by a bunch of first years.

I was a nervous, apprehensive kid, a worrier. If I wasn't worried I'd be worried that everything was going too well so sought something to be worried about. Despite being well received at Mackie, for some weeks I still had the skits when I got ready for school. Inexplicable really, I wasn't bullied, I had friends, teachers took to me, I think I'd built up a false image in my mind that moving schools from Birmingham in England to Stonehaven in Scotland was such an upheaval that the world would turn upside down and I'd have to re-acclimatise, as if on another planet. I was catastrophizing, fearing the worst, getting myself worked up over something that I needn't have. To everyone else, kids and teachers alike, I was just another school-kid, they had their own lives to get on with and had better things to do than devise ways to make my life uncomfortable. By the new school year in August '82, four months after I'd joined Mackie, I was fine. By then we'd moved from rented accommodation in Aberdeen to Salmon Lane and enjoyed a full summer break, Stonehaven was beginning to feel like home.

What else can I tell you about Mackie in the early eighties? Well the three sports teachers were Mr Bruce (a coiled spring), Mr Hay (owner of a slim ferret housed on his upper lip) and Mr Montgomery (gave me two laps of the field for using my hockey stick like a golf club). Sports lessons could be brutal, thanks chiefly to the weather, the perishing cold piercing our puny frames. Brucie would be spewing forth instructions, barely audible above the howling wind, while we stood rooted to the spot, shivering as our legs turned blue. I was in the school football team run by English teacher, Mr Taylor, who assembled a decent side despite kitting us out in a pseudo Wolverhampton

Wanderers strip. I played at right back behind a brick outhouse of a midfielder called Malcolm Durward (Minnie) who once put a block tackle in on a Hazelhead Academy opponent, twice his size, that moved Aberdeen six inches closer to Stonehaven. Absolutely fearless he was, from Kineff I think. Away games were great, we'd be excused from the final lesson of the day and pile onto a bus feeling like kings, but home matches on our exposed field behind the school, with the wind whipping around our legs, would fair chatter the teeth.

History was taken by Mr Gibson who wore a perpetual grin regardless of his mood, very disconcerting. He'd sound off at you, threatening to dust his belt off, while smirking throughout, we knew he'd wouldn't belt us really though, he was too nice a guy for that. Mr Somerville took Modern Studies and was a very definite, serious kind of chap who seemingly put hours into preparing his lessons. He wore corduroy trousers, long sleeved checked shirts, tank tops and suede jesus boots, I imagined him attending 'right on' socialist marches or leafleting unsuspecting districts of the Grampians with left wing material. He loved politics and spoke passionately about it, particularly apartheid in South Africa which he had an encyclopaedic knowledge of. His teaching style was to open with a lengthy, uninterrupted monologue before leaving us to scribble away in silence while he buried his nose in books and broadsheets. He stood no messing, it only needed a glare over his horn rimmed glasses to shut us up. Who else was there? I can't remember his name but the English teacher taught us about Lewis Grassic Gibbon with an infectious enthusiasm while struggling to reign in his obvious disdain for the English. Another teacher, 'Ock', was of advancing years, very old school, a burly bloke with a deep voice that boomed down corridors as he pursued miscreants. He'd pull one side of his suit jacket aside so you could see the four pronged leather strap hanging over his shoulder but he never used it other than as a deterrent, so kids continued to play him up. Another teacher, Mr Douglas, used to threaten the belt on you but everyone knew he wouldn't use it... or so we thought until the fateful day that I proved otherwise.

We had several names for receiving the belt, an instrument of corporal punishment that was later outlawed. 'Yer gettin' whipped,' or, 'tonged' would be the most common reference to an imminent belting with the accompanying 'fer... .tsch!' sound effect mouthed by excitable pupils when a furious teacher beckoned you forward. It was a punishment to fear for good reason, bloody sore it was. The deed would be carried out thus; the *whippee* would hold outstretched fingers across the palm of his other hand while the *whipper* stood a pace directly in front of the *whippee* before lashing the belt, from great height, down across the *whippee's* fingers. Two strokes was the norm, four if you had done something heinous and six if the teacher was a borderline sadist. Either way, you couldn't feel your fingers afterwards or zip up your anorak for a week. I took my beating from Mr Douglas in front of a wide-eyed classroom of fellow pupils and was joined in my punishment by Paul Crandon and a hapless first year who's name I don't know. We'd had a deluge of snow in recent days and received strict instructions at morning assembly not to throw snowballs. As we walked between lessons, we left the school's main building and headed for the annexe, where Mr Douglas's room lay. There was a thirty yard walk during which Paul and I pummelled this first year with snowballs as he strode ahead of us, all the time, unbeknown to us, being watched through the window by Mr Douglas. Just as the first year kid reached the annexe, he finally snapped, scooped up a line of snow from the handrail and chucked a feeble effort in our direction by way of brave retaliation. It plopped apologetically into the snow halfway between he and us, but he too was spotted by Douglas and got whipped aswell. Poor chap.

A gungy, I became aware, was the hoisting into the air of some poor unfortunate by the waist band of his underpants, or of course the double gungy, being lifted both front and back simultaneously. I managed to avoid the indignity of the gungy but witnessed several, including one which resulted in Mincey dangling from a cloakroom peg by the waistband of his garish orange underpants. Most uncomfortable viewing, but I'd sooner view it than experience it.

In my early days at Mackie, I kicked around with a boy called Craig Malcolm who was a bundle of energy, he lived on Carron Terrace but may have moved away from Stonehaven shortly afterwards if I remember right. Next I hooked up with a group of lads I'd spend the remainder of my school years with. I had two circles of friends (ooh, get me), there were my school friends and my golf club friends, two distinctly separate camps that didn't cross over in any respect. I wouldn't say my golfing buddies blanked me at school but we didn't share time either, our friendship confined solely to the Stonehaven Golf Club arena where we spent thousands of hours together. Keith Douglas and his brother Jack, Bryan Innes, Bruce Ferguson, Frank McCarron, David Ross were the leading lights in the teenage golfing 'set', we devoted entire summer holidays, weekends and after school evenings to our golf, the thriving

27

junior section run by Andy Locke's father, Gordon. We were largely of equal standard, similar humour, same age within a few months and fought hard in every competition. At school I became firm friends with a guy called Jason Waddleton, something of a hero with the girls given he was singer in a band, wore an ear stud and had short spiky hair. He also started shaving miles before anyone else (I started at nineteen, he at six) so was an all round cool dude, why he befriended me I don't know, our shared passion for Auf Wiedershen Pet probably playing a major role. We were both English kids recently moved to Stonehaven so had a kinship, and when the hit series *Auf Wiederschen Pet* came out starring characters from our native North East England and Birmingham, we clung onto it as if it were a dear friend. My golfing friends were all locals, my school friends however were mostly English lads who'd moved up to Scotland (Jason, Paul Crandon, Dick) and we formed a bond, although never to the exclusion of locals, we rubbed along nicely with Stoney's natives, I think they found us a novelty at first but then accepted us as regular blokes once they'd got to know us.

My walk to school would take about twenty minutes, Mackie Academy being at the top of the town and our house near the bottom, the house on the beach on Salmon Lane. It was a grim slog uphill until I learned to time my stroll up Ann Street to coincide with Bruce Ferguson's emergence from his house and the kind offer of a lift from his Mum. Sometimes I'd be too late or early so would climb the steep entry to Slug Road and push on until the road became less arduous as it reached the small green opposite Mansell Avenue. There were a hundred routes to school from the auld toon, I'd vary it depending on mood, weather or friends. If it was dry and still I'd walk up Ann Street and then the length of the Slugger. If it was windy and wet I'd wander through the Market Square, past Larnoch's chippy, along Robert Street to the St Leonards Hotel and up to the Heugh before turning right up to the school. I somehow felt protected from the driving rain when dawdling this route. If I was walking up with Jim Acton there'd be a different route every time, sometimes burrowing through folk's gardens, and if I was meeting Jason I'd walk up to Arduthie Road and meet him there. Then a mistake, I decided to take my bike instead, three accidents later, all on Slug Road, battered and bruised, I conceded defeat and started getting the bus with my bus money instead of pocketing it to buy yum-yums from Strathdee.

Two of the accidents weren't my fault, the other, the worst one, was. You know when you're travelling fast downhill, running, sledging, cycling, whatever, and you reach a point when you realise you're completely out of control? Well that was me one warm afternoon after school as I cycled home in a hurry to get back to my snooker table. Screaming down the hill from the Heugh and having negotiated the two bends before you get to the small green opposite the Gordon's house, I suddenly realised the pedals were circling way faster than they should. The chain had come off so all of the tension had gone out of the pedals and my feet were pushing fresh air, I felt like Roadrunner. I looked down, lost concentration on the road, and unintentionally dug the toes of my right foot into the tarmac, halting the front wheel in its tracks and sending the rear wheel up into the air with me perched on the saddle. I wasn't perched on the saddle for long. At breakneck speed, I flew over the handlebars a distance of fifteen feet, stretched my hands out to protect my fall and gambolled down the road in a whirlwind of arms and legs. My hands and elbows were cut to ribbons, my head was split open and I lay in a state of shock. Don't know what happened next except blue lights were involved. There was no lasting damage but let's just say it smarted a little. The other two occasions I hereby blame the motoring public of Stonehaven for, both times I was cycling straightforwardly along Slug Road, again after school, only to be taken out by cars driven by oblivious drivers as they pulled out from off roads on the left. One of these drivers was a teacher but I won't embarrass her by saying who, my knee dented the driver's door before I landed on the bonnet, no harm done other than to her pride and my breeks. The other collision was frightening though, I'd climbed the hill, reached the junction outside the Heugh and was all set to rocket down the slope the other side, when an elderly driver pulled out on me. My bike went under the car, I was sprawled out over the bonnet and he kept driving, slowly, my bike wedged under his engine. The hellish screech as my bike was carried slowly forward was deafening and he stopped only when the lollipop lady walked out in front of him. He was in a state of shock and hadn't taken his foot off the accelerator, when he did I was despatched to the road, sliding down his car bonnet onto the floor like a scene from the Wacky Races. A passer by scraped me off the road, sat me on a low wall but let go of his shaken, jelly legged patient who promptly fell backwards into a rose bush. To say my fellow Mackie pupils weren't sympathetic is an understatement, they gawped and guffawed while I struggled to my feet, dignified it was not. The driver couldn't have been more apologetic and delivered some sweets to me when he found out where I lived, he was into his eighties and I believe stopped driving after that. I returned to Shank's Pony and the bus.

Then, in the Autumn of 1986 after four years living in Stonehaven, I left town. It all happened so suddenly.

I'd achieved middling results in my three Highers, nowhere near enough to qualify for university, something my peers had accomplished. This was fine by me, I was still a boy really, barely seventeen and nowhere near mature enough to live away from home. I enrolled for another couple of Highers in sixth form and saw out the summer playing golf. What I didn't know was that my father had other plans for me.

I was your stereotypical stroppy teenager, wanting nothing to do with my parents other than to treat them dismissively, particularly my father. I was a nightmare to have around the house, grumpy and self-centred, full of an attitude that sapped the energy around me. Difficult, argumentative, passive aggressive, nothing was good enough, I was angry with the world but didn't know why, despite living a cossetted, molly cuddled existence. Stonehaven was too sleepy I announced, I wanted to return to Birmingham, that's to say to my deluded perception of Birmingham, a place where I could attend Villa matches, enjoy the city lights and live a little.

My father was tired of my demoralising behaviour, he also felt another year plodding through school would not be beneficial for me. So, in an act of brinkmanship, he made a couple of calls to Birmingham Polytechnic and found me a place on a Business Studies HND course. 'You said you wanted back to Birmingham, here's your chance.'

I was cornered, couldn't back out and was gone within a fortnight. A whirlwind of financial planning later, they had student grants in those days, and I was in the passenger seat of my Mum's car waving adios to Stonehaven. Eight hours later she dropped me off at Gorway campus in Walsall and left. I was absolutely terrified.

If I had my time again I'd have stayed put and spent another year at Mackie, weighing up my options. I'd swallow my pride and concede to my parents that I was nowhere near ready to leave home. But the notion had run away with itself and in the blink of an eye I was transported from the safe, cushy life of a homeboy to an intimidating, frightening existence as a trainee adult. I was young, naïve and scared. My response was to drink. More of that later.

CHAPTER FIVE

'Let me take you down...'
The Beatles

B ut enough reminiscing, let's get back to the golf. Before I go any further with the travails of the SGC winter league, I'd better give you a description of this golf course of ours.

1st

I love the first. Behind the green, which lies three hundred yards away, stretches a backdrop of endless blue, the elevated tee providing spectacular views of the epic North Sea, Stonehaven bay and the wider coastline beyond, beautiful.

There's no future to the right, the cliffs beckon your ball to the beach below, so make sure you're straight, or left, where there's bags of room. There are three staging posts along the fairway; the humps, the corner post and Hitler's Bunker. The rite of passage for any young golfer is to graduate over time from driving the ball past the humps 160 yards away, then the corner post another 20 yards further and eventually Hitler's Bunker, about 20 yards again. Once you become a manny it's possible to drive the green, but the fairway narrows so if you're at all off target you'll either bung it out of bounds or into the two bunkers protecting the green either side. The humps are three small hilly hummocks sat in the middle of the fairway, the corner post is a white stick signalling out of bounds on the right side of the hole, and Hitler's is a crevice on the left side of the fairway created by a Second World War bomb. Fact.

The entrance to the green is sloped. Many's the time your floated pitch sails through the air with you licking your lips in anticipation of a birdie putt, only for the ball to thump the downslope and skitter through the back of the green. You have to judge the distance well or bump and run a seven iron, hoping it teeters at the top of the slope before rolling down to the holeside. Thin it through the back and you'll drop into a trough that surrounds the green, thin it with knobs on and you disappear out of bounds. The greenside bunkers are shallow, you shouldn't struggle to flop the ball out. The green itself isn't overly undulated, a comfortable two putt awaits.

2nd

Cracking hole this, stroll off it with a par on your card and you feel like cock of the walk. It's a near on 200 yard par three so you need to connect with a good 'un off the tee, don't top it or you're history, there's a deep cliff lined ravine stretching between you and the next section of terra firma. The sheer drop continues all along the right hand side of the hole, the cliffs welcoming any kind of slice before feeding the ball down to the shore to drown in the North Sea.

The tee is set back behind the first green and, even more effectively than the first, offers beautiful views of the sea and Stonehaven Bay. Frankly it's an underused vantage point, early into the round you're concentrating on your golf, trying to get the scorecard off to a good start, attractive views are at the back of your mind, at the forefront are images of smooth swings and clean connections. But try and take time to marvel at the beauty of nature from the second tee, its awe inspiring and will help you forget the double bogey you might have racked up moments earlier.

The green is raised high above the fairway, any ball landing short will stop in its tracks or roll back down the bank. Your tee shot needs to carry to the green therefore, and at nearly two hundred yards that's a tough ask. The majority of players find themselves pitching up from the bank below, that's if they've avoided the bunkers. There are four traps, two small ones set twenty yards in front of the green welcoming short ranged tee shots and one either side of the dancefloor, like a pair of ears attached to a wide face. The green itself is shallow, it's very difficult to keep your drive upon it unless you've parachuted in from outer space. There's a shelf behind the green arresting plenty of balls journeying toward the steep upward slope beyond, if you find yourself in this little gully don't thin your pitch or you'll be playing your next shot from below the aforementioned bank at the front.

The putting surface slopes from back to front, beware the steeper than envisaged borrows and it's slick, a very three puttable green.

3rd

The third and fourth holes are best described as a gateway to the splendour ahead. The third in particular offering little joy, see the survey later in this book, and that's down to the steeply sloped fairway which falls almost vertically from left to right. Indeed there's almost no fairway in the truest sense since to cut the grass short would be to guarantee any straight drive rolls down to the fence running along the right hand side. So the grass is left long to ensure drives remain in play but this means players are forced to stoop when addressing their second shot with the ball lying below their feet. Still, every course has its idiosyncrasies and once you've embraced Stoney's quirks, you're set fair.

The grassy humps residing a hundred yards up the 1st hole are mirrored on the 3rd, failing to clear them from the tee is equally reprehensible and those incapable of so doing must play their second shot with trousers around their ankles. A decent drive leaves a short iron to the flat green ahead, raised above the adjacent slope on the right, if you miss the green on that side and are yet to perfect the Mickelson flop shot, you're on your way to a double. The green welcomes balls gathering from the bank on the left and since there's little chance of parking your approach in the small bunker up there, unless you're particularly wild, you can bail left without panic.

A bunker lies behind the green to receive thinners and is a bugger to get out of, avoid at all costs. The green is symptomatic of all Stonehaven greens, a true roll with subtle borrows insisting on your full attention or you'll be stomping off to the next tee bemoaning a three stab.

4th

A blind tee shot, another grassy hillock a hundred yards away, a blind second shot and a chance of being peppered by balls straying from the 16th tee, the 4th is not the jewel in Stonehaven's crown. There's a sharply elevated green with a cheeky bail out bunker to the left, the green's a perfect square and it's a long walk to the 5th tee particularly if you need to gather yourself following a double bogey. Let's get off the this hole and move on. Nobody's favourite this one.

5th

A spectacular hole with a treat of a sea view from tee and green. You drive off next to the railway line and can't resist a peek at the scattering of golf balls lying tantalisingly on the track, don't be tempted to sneak over the fence to retrieve them though, that's a hanging offence (if you haven't already been flattened by an express train).

Between you and the green sits a deep gully awaiting receipt of your drive. If you're prone to a scuffed teeshot, do it here, because it gives you an excuse to play a dramatic second shot across the valley below. Best not put your approach right, it's curtains with OB beckoning, go left and it's bunker time, go long and you're in the scrub. It's an expansive green, there's no excuse for missing it really. I've always wondered why this hole merits a stroke index of two, there are several tougher holes lying in wait.

6th

A blind par three, a member's hole given you need to pick the correct line off the tee. But before you thrash your drive away, if it's a calm day, take a minute to check out the dolphins leaping in the sea behind you, they tend to congregate here occasionally. I remember Keith Douglas looking for his ball behind this tee once, his drive from the medal tees smacked the yellow tee box in front and careered back over his shoulder. Priceless. He denies it, but he would.

Sliced tee shots on the 6th either drift out of bounds or wipe out the players standing on the 7th tee. A pull left takes you towards the bunkers and if you're straight but short, you've got a nasty raised ledge to negotiate. Tip – once you've driven, watch for the reaction from players on the 7th tee for an estimation of your ball's proximity to the hole. If they quickly swing their heads around in your direction it's looking good, if they don't there's nothing for you to get excited about.

7th

I adore this hole. Picture those golfing calendars with improbable golf holes located in awe inspiring mountains and cliff edges around the world, well here you have a genuine article. 170 yards from tee to green separated almost entirely by a huge valley with the cliffs falling away to the right. And what an awesome view as the sea stretches away from Skatie Shore beneath. It's out of bounds on the right and don't bother trying to retrieve your ball unless you're prepared to risk an untimely death falling from the cliff edge. If you're lucky, a gorse bush will interrupt your fall and leave you hanging until a helicopter rescues you.

It's a helluva climb from tee to green but here we arrive at the nub of playing golf at Stonehaven Golf Club. Yes, it's hilly, you will encounter uneven stances and have a choice of either embracing it or taking up snooker, quit the whinging or quit your round. In the wintertime, once you're up on the exposed greenside, you might lose the feeling in your hands. In the summer though, you can put a parasol out and enjoy the rays. Either way, concentrate on your putting because this green is rapid.

8th

Jewel of a hole this, a short par three with a bowl shaped target area providing an amphitheatre of a green. The putting surface is tricky, it's severe with hidden undulations and it falls away to the front so don't be short off the tee or the ball will just keep coming back to you. The banking surrounding the left side and back of the green can be used to feed the ball down to the hole but don't get cocky, if you strike your ball too far left you'll simply get tangled up in the tufty stuff or be left standing on the ledge looking like a prize leek. There's a pot bunker to the right for those tempted to arrive from that angle. This beautiful hole is a tougher proposition off the back tees when you'll be fishing a medium iron out of your bag instead of a short iron, what appears a simple par three is far from it when playing against the wind off the medals.

9th

And now we reach 'the field', a four hole stretch situated the other side of the railway line. Entry to the field is not over the tracks, your trolley wheels might get wedged between the rails as a train advances. Visitors would not be attracted to the club if they learned players diced with death halfway through their round, Russian Roulette should be kept within the confines of war films and not carried out while wearing casual golfing slacks and a tartan Tammy. The membership stats would sure take a pounding if members were routinely wiped out by 100mph trains innocently travelling to Aberdeen. No, there's a small archway beneath the bridge for you to trundle through instead.

The 9th is a longish par four by Stoney standards. Unless you're an animal off the tee, you'll have a long iron for your second shot provided you've cleared the hill with your blind tee shot, just sail it over the marker post and you're in business. (The number of times folk ask 'what's the line?' on this tee is remarkable considering a hulking great black and white marker post glares at them from the top of the hill). There's plenty of room out to the right but pull it left and you're OB unless it ricochets off the Inverness – Penzance intercity express.

The fairway flattens out beyond the hill, giving sight of the relatively narrow entrance to the green between two bunkers. A plantation of trees, not enough to be labelled a forest, more of a forest-ette, lies to the right from a distance of sixty yards in. It's a magnet for sliced golf balls unless you do a proper job and land it onto the adjacent 12th hole, from where a lofted gap wedge will see you onto the dance floor unless you fluff it into the middle of the trees, there speaks the voice of experience.

10th

Another blind tee shot, the target being the highest point of the hill from where you can enjoy an awesome view of Stonehaven bay, Dunnotter Castle is visible a little distance beyond. It's a wide open fairway, the railway line on the left needs a ludicrous hook if you're to trouble it.

This hole used to get us into trouble as junior members. We'd throw down a dozen balls at the top of the hill and loft them onto the green, leaving a carpet of pitchmarks. It's a long green but narrow, if you miss it you're left with a nervy lob shot back up onto the green and if you overshoot it you're OB in the foundations of a house currently being built. Either side of the green's entrance lie bunkers which are only too pleased to welcome misguided bump and runs from golfers too frightened to risk the aerial route. Once you're on the green it's very flat and true, three putts are a criminal offence here, no excuse.

11th

Cheeky hole this one, well designed with a two tiered green. To your immediate left is oblivion stretching all the way to the green, any pull or hook is rewarded with a reload. The green is drivable for big hitters but tweak it a little left and there's no future. Only greed will take you out of bounds, there's bags of room on the right, that said, your knees turn to jelly when you're on the tee and conscious of a hooking issue in your game. Aim well right and you'll be fine unless you bladder it straight as a die and disappear into the aforementioned forest-ette by the 9th green.

From the fairway it's a pleasurable pitch to the green but make sure you select the right tier or you're in three putt country. Green side bunkers catch drifting approach shots and there's also a fairway bunker on the left which can be a blessing when you've careered one towards the OB. Good players expect a birdie here.

12th

The 12th is my nemesis. Stroke index one, a long par four with a blind approach. Your tee shot, if well struck, will lie halfway up a banked rising from where you cannot see the green. You will walk up the hill to choose a line upon which to aim but the moment you return to stand over your ball, you start thinking about insurance, 'I'll just fire it a little bit further right so I don't go OB on the left.' Halfway through your downswing your body tells you that, just to be certain, perhaps further right still would be a safer bet so by the time your club face connects with your ball you're bailing out to a patch of no mans land below the green. You now have an awkward lob shot over a bunker which you'll either fluff with a horrible decel or thin into the semi rough. Three shots later you're walking off with a six. Every bleedin' time.

13th

The 13th signals the beginning of Stonehaven's 'gully', a run of three holes played over and upon opposite sides of a ravine. The first of this trio is a short par four requiring a decent connection off the tee or you'll be reloading having dumped your ball in one of a hundred gorse bushes. The carry is around 130 yards whereupon you reach a sloped fairway which feeds from top left to bottom right, where the 14th green lies. Common etiquette is to wait until the 14th green clears before you attempt your 13th tee shot, it doesn't do to kneecap fellow golfers.

Hoick your drive left and you're on the railway line, shove it right and you're down the cliff's edge, but nail it straight and the green is reachable. Most of us, deliberately or otherwise, leave a short pitch up to the green which is difficult to execute and easy to muff. The green, like so many at Stoney, has bunkers either side of the front, and is relatively flat after a slightly sloped entrance. There's another bunker at the back collecting skittered pitches.

This is the most birdieable hole on the course if you get a good drive away, but take a breath before you hit your second shot, after the yomp around the dirt track and up cardiac hill you'll need to gather yourself. It feels like you've had three rounds with Mike Tyson.

14th

A blind par three of only 120 yards but you try getting a three on it, cos I can't. The elevated tee requires you to aim at a terrifically tall marker post rooted behind the green but everyone bails right knowing the fate of any ball heading left (the cliffs).

Bunkers await your arrival on the right side, three of them in a line, and if you push it even further right you've a nasty pitch to negotiate. Land it short, expecting it to run onto the green, and it may grow legs to disappear off the back, overshoot the green and you're down the gully. It's a wide green yet still a relatively narrow target given the danger either side.

You'll sometimes experience a traffic jam on the 14th as golfers politely give it the 'after you Claude'. Folk driving off the 13th tee wait for those on the 13th fairway to stand aside, simultaneously the putters on the 14th green are required to pause in case the tee shots head their way. Players who've teed off at the adjacent 15th can't walk down the path until the drivers off the 13th tee have played so now you have up to sixteen people waiting and wondering what the protocol is, lots of waving of hands, beckoning, huffing and puffing before the traffic splutters back into life. It's a little unseemly but a good excuse to blame someone other than yourself if you hit a bad shot, 'it was a' that waitin.'

15th

Now we reach what the majority of members regard as the signature hole, the 15th. It is a beauty, a challenge whatever the weather, a nine iron with a following wind but a driver if the wind's gusting against you. 150 yards long, this is the trip back across the gully you crossed when playing the 13th. You don't want to leave it short, there's no future landing it in the gully, your ball will be lost or unplayable, but if you scramble it within ten yards of the green you've found the close cropped apron. The long putting surface is bordered by bunkers either side and a bank at the back which you'd sooner clear than rest upon, or you have an awkward pitch. Landing right of the green, adjacent to the bunker, leaves you a tricky lob shot and to send your drive too far left is death by a thousand gorse bushes.

Back on the tee, exposed to the battering wind, there stands the original clubhouse chimney breast, dating back to 1888. The course had a different layout back then with a green below on Skatie Shore. My father marked the centenary with a hole-in-one here, a bit of useless information for you, but at least it guarantees my Dad will buy this book.

16th

The gully duly negotiated, it's time for the three homeward holes beginning with the course's only par five which runs alongside the railway line. Compared to the 17th it's a relatively level fairway with bags of room to the left, you can sling your drive onto the 4th fairway which runs parallel, much more preferable than pushing it OB onto the railway track. Crack a good 'un away and you can reach the green in two, but you'll need to be extremely accurate if you're to hit the dance floor through the eye of a needle. Chances are you'll fall short or drift left towards the 17th tee from where you'll need to pitch up to the raised green. If you are brave enough to send the ball towards the right side of the green, risking the railway line, there's a bunker to catch your fall. Decent players expect a birdie here, worse than six demands a written explanation.

17th

My least favourite hole on the golf course lies parallel to my second least (3rd), both on the side of a steep slope offering nothing but an uneven stance from which to play your pitch. If you bladder your drive you can reach this par four's green, but you'll need to set it off high on the right side and hope it bumbles down off the steep bank to the desired destination. If you don't make the green you're better off finishing low on the left, you can float a lob wedge then rather than blade one from the steeper slope above. Again the green is very true but with hidden undulations that members are yet to fathom. In truth, a hole to tick off your scorecard and move on.

18th

The closing hole is a cracker. 180 yard par three which plays much longer on windy days, a welcoming green but heavily bunkered, a picturesque, centuries old graveyard sitting alongside, very apt considering some scorecards submitted. The sloped fairway encourages you to aim rightwards so the ball feeds down to the green but you'd be surprised how resolutely balls cling to the bank, refusing to obey barked orders from the tee to 'frickin' well come down then!'. Better to land it on the front with a high trajectory, easier said than done. The green is deceptively quick, three putt territory for sure.

The clubhouse and car park overlook the 18th so if you're going to make a dog's breakfast of a hole don't make it this one. A common fault is to leave your tee shot short and right, high on the bank, muff your pitch onto the fringe, charge your putt past the hole, miss the return and walk off with an ugly five to the amusement of clubhouse onlookers.

CHAPTER SIX

'I know it's over and it never really began'
The Smiths

It's a frustrating caper the Winter League. You spend the week getting all revved up only for inclement weather to close the damned course. They don't suffer this in Florida, the only danger over there is a lack of water with which to hydrate sun bathed players, or suspension of play because the sun's too bright. Oh for a winter league abroad, to sign your scorecard sitting in shorts on the veranda instead of shivering beneath five layers of clothing, your pen full of frozen ink.

That's two weekends running I've missed my golf, first due to water logging after a monsoon and second because the course had morphed into an ice rink. In truth, it's probably for the best, an enforced break can only do my game, and Keith's sanity, good. If Villa's strikers couldn't hit a cow's arse with a banjo then, right now, neither can I with a golf club. Every cloud has a silver lining (once it's finished depositing its contents on Stonehaven Golf Club) and my rest from golf might bring back a new me. I was watching Rory McIlroy play a tournament in Dubai at the weekend (on the telly like) and spotted something in his game that I just might put into practice myself. To let you into a secret, he was standing up to his tee shot, swinging his club through the ball and despatching it 320 yards down the middle. Buoyed by this discovery, I propose to replicate it when next I have the chance. And they say watching telly's bad for you, pah!

CHAPTER SEVEN

'I'm lost among the undergrowth'
Manic Street Preachers

With another weekend's golf cancelled due to inclement weather, I turned my attention towards finishing my tutorial, How To Knife Pitches & Influence Scorecards, in which I present a masterclass in short game ineptitude. It had been many years in the making but I now completed the final write up.

Preparation is key. Any duffer worth his salt must pretend to be half decent even if they wouldn't recognise one end of a club from another. So 1) tuck your golf glove into your back pocket with the fingers dangling out like the pro's do, 2) hitch your jersey's sleeves halfway up your forearms and 3) get down on your haunches to study the contours between your ball and the pin (even though you'll be taking the undulations out of play with a jet speed thinner).

Now to the shot itself. Remember three key words; stance, tempo and contact.

Starting with *stance*. For maximum effect, you must ensure the ball is played off your front foot. Any temptation to play it from the middle of your stance, or worse, from the back foot, brings into play the possibility of a conventional, lofted pitch resulting in an arced trajectory enabling the ball to drop like a stone near the flag. Instead, you must play off the front foot ensuring the clubface is so far advanced in your swing's follow through that you virtually miss the ball altogether.

Next we'll look at *tempo*. It is absolutely imperative that your swing has all the composure of a cat on a hot tin roof escaping the fevered attention of a bull mastiff. You must exhibit frayed nerves and a very obvious lack of confidence, as if this were the first golf shot of your entire life. Draw the club back in a deliberate fashion, pretending for all the world that everything is under control, then begin a jerky downswing before the backswing has actually been completed. And here is the key. You must now accelerate the pace to turbo charge, frantically lurching at the ball as if it had just insulted your granny. As you approach the ball at breakneck speed, dip both knees nervously, wear an anguished facial expression and show a look of terror that confirms you want to get this wretched manoeuvre out of the way as quickly as possible.

Now we've reached the moment of truth, the *connection*, the final act in this helpless demonstration of short game buffoonery. By now your hands, arms, torso and legs should be utterly out of synch with one another and past the point of no return. Your hands will be behind the ball as you present the clubface at entirely the wrong angle, halfway up the spherical object before you, your shoulders should be rising prematurely causing the club to rise six inches higher and your sphincter ought to be twitching furiously. Lean all of your weight onto your right foot and, instead of allowing the loft of the clubface to do the work, attempt a wristy flick, as if planning to slam dunk the ball from the heavens.

Your clubface should now be in the perfect position not to meet the back of the golf ball where it junctions with the turf, but three quarters of the way up instead. This way you can be assured of the classic knee height knifing, your ball travelling like an exocet across the green, your playing partners scurrying for cover. As you follow through, maintain the look of terror and prepare for a sharp pain in your right hand as you thin the ball to within an inch of its life. Upon impact look up, forcing yourself to watch the full horror of your handiwork as the ball careers through the dancefloor and skips into the scruff at the back of the green. Look to the skies, close your eyes and wish you were somewhere else in the world before trudging to the rear of the green to continue the torture. Standard practice from hereon is to somehow nurdle the ball onto the putting surface, race your bogey putt past and end up with a triple.

Congratulations! You have perfected the kneecap knifer, the hand wringing thinner that means, despite being greenside after two shots, you've walked off with a seven. Repeat this farrago several times in the round, march directly from the 18th green to the changing room toilets, slam the trap door, sit on the throne and weep gently into the crook of your arm.

Next week – *How To Shank Your Putts.*

CHAPTER EIGHT

'You'll have to come up with something better than that'
The Wedding Present

Round 3 – December 5th 2015

Welcome to round three of the Russon/Douglas winter league pantomime. While the morning starters enjoyed dry and benign conditions, we spent the entire round wearing full waterproofs in unrelenting rain and back nine fog. Thankfully however, one of us was up for the fight... but the less said about the other herbert the better.

Keith greeted me on the first tee with his familiarly grudging grunt.

'How you doing?' I ventured.

'Canna believe you talked me into this winter league sh*te', came the reply.

'Looking forward to the game?' I countered.

'Nae really, could'na hink o onyhin worse.'

Upon such inspirational exchanges are successful partnerships made.

Little did I know that Keith's mood had in fact peaked and would worsen from this point on. Brandishing a brand new Titleist Pro-V, he proudly showed me a red sheep he'd diligently drawn upon it with a red stubby, in tribute to his Sheepo nickname. Thankfully he'd taken a photo of his ball because he'd never see it again, ten seconds later the object was making its way down the cliff to the north sea, a horrible slice sending it to a watery death. His language ripened as he skulked back towards the ball pocket of his bag for a reload while I turned my attention towards my opening drive. As a portent of things to come, I duly drilled mine down the middle to within a flick of the green, taking care of business while my partner fluffed his lines. Every partnership has a dominant character and a follower, first string and second string, today Keith was to be, and pardon the vulgarity, my bitch. He might play off a handicap of four and be renowned for steady golf, but sometimes it needs something a little more than 'meat and potatoes' play to sort the wheat from the chaff, so I decided to take the bull by the horns and deliver some fireworks (not literally, that would be ludicrous, riding into Stoney on the back of a bull with rockets fizzing out of my pockets? No thanks).

Cometh the hour, cometh the man. With conditions at Dreichter Scale 10, my partner could only stand back in wonder as I brought the first eight holes to its knees, birdieing 7 and 8 while parring the majority of others with a nonchalance that made a mockery of my 10 handicap. I hoped this might inspire Keith to a higher level but not a bit of it, he was playing second fiddle so loudly that the club captain marched onto the course and asked him to turn the sound down. His streaky par on 9 provided only his second contribution to our scorecard (I'd deliberately three putted the 3rd to allow him some of the limelight) and the back nine evidenced a similarly unequal distribution of contribution. By the time we reached the 16th it was becoming a little embarrassing, I was having to instigate conversation about the weather just to deflect attention from his pathetic inability to bring anything of value to the party, apart from holding the flag while I putted. There was a particularly awkward moment as we left the 15th green, he verbalised dissatisfaction at having to mark the scorecard all the way round, I suggested that it was the least he could do given I was providing the numbers to be recorded. I was doing the business, he wasn't. Had the roles been reversed and I were marking his scores instead, we'd have been facing the indignity of a three digit total. It was a one man show for sure.

Keith's behaviour deteriorated as the round progressed, due chiefly to the humiliation he was suffering, so, to improve the atmosphere, I kindly waited for him to hole his lengthy birdie putt on the 16th before nudging in my own two footer, this way he could mark the birdie down as his own and not mine. Order was restored on the final two holes however, as I notched two solid pars while Keith arsed around like a complete beginner, plonking his drive onto the railway line at 17 and shoving his tee shot on 18 closer to the clubhouse than the green.

So to summarise, a gross 65 was achieved in abominable conditions before we adjourned to the bar for a hard earned drink which Keith rightly purchased, the least he could do. I congratulated him on the neatness of his handwriting, the card looked very pretty with all of those low numbers I'd provided. 'F*ck off Russon' came his reply. This is what I enjoy most about the winter league, the warm camaraderie. As he drifted back to his motor, with his tail between his legs, I bid him farewell but politely asked him to get a touch of practice before our next outing. I have to say his response wasn't encouraging, standing as he did with the same number of fingers in the air as he had lost Sheepo motiffed golf balls during the afore mentioned, error strewn round.

CHAPTER NINE

'Everyone knows he looks daft'
The Wedding Present

Round 4 – December 13th 2015

After the fireworks of round three it was back to humdrum golf for the first half of round four, we couldn't get anything going. Conditions were ideal, not a breath of wind, no rain, only zero temperatures spoiled it. Keith's brother, Jack, joined us, he was limbering up for a game at The Old Course the following day. He trudged the first seventeen holes with us before bailing out, the 18th at Stoney claiming another victim unprepared to make the climb from the green back up to the locker room.

Jack casually birdied the 1st hole to take the honour, only to dump two balls out on the 2nd, I'd instantly dragged him down to my level after a shocker of an opening hole myself. His presence was important, not for his sparkling repartee, although that's always a bonus, but Keith and I needed a referee following the previous week's argy bargy. Keith continued to complain about my unwillingness to replace flagsticks before vacating greens, twenty eight consecutive holes so he reckoned. Which brings me to a letter I received in the post following our previous game, a letter accusing me of 'shameful bias' when writing up an account of our last round upon the blog I'd been keeping, bigging up my own performance while deriding my partner's efforts. I won't embarrass the letter's author by revealing his identity, so let's just refer to his surname, Douglas. No, on second thoughts, we'll just call him by his Christian name, Keith.

The letter was rather rude, accusing me of undermining the efforts my partner had made the previous week, at least I think that was the gist, I could barely decipher the childlike handwriting, poor grammar and diabolical spelling. Anyhow, I brought this letter up with Keith as we walked along the first fairway…

'We really ought to rediscover the harmony in this partnership Keith' I suggested. 'After all, there's no 'I' in team.'

'Aye, but there is in prick' was his response.

We soldiered on despite our differences, exchanging pars until blotting the copybook with bogeys on the 6th and 9th. It was the 11th before our first birdie but we handed that advantage straight back with a bogey on 12. It's a shame I didn't take my camera, you should have seen Jack's headgear, a bright red skin tight head sock that looked like a cross between a bandana and a prophylactic. Standing on the 14th tee he looked like Charlie Chan, the head sock stretching his eyelids skywards, all he needed was the fake moustache.

I'd lost patience with Keith's crap golf by the time we reached the gully, so decided to take control of the situation. I birdied 14, drained a lengthy par putt on 15 and slammed in a birdie on 17. No messing. Someone needed to take charge and thankfully my efforts shamed Keith into upping his game, he birdied 16 and despite his best efforts, avoided a three putt on the last to notch a closing par. We ended with a 65, not earth shattering but respectable, a decent day's work in contrast to my football team (Aston Villa) who were playing Arsenal at precisely the same time. We shared two goals with them but weren't at all greedy with our share, let's put it that way. We were overly generous in actual fact. 15 games, 6 points, we're goin down and no mistake. As for the golf, I'm taking my A game next weekend, watch out for an eye bleeding score.

CHAPTER TEN

'The North wind keeps picking up speed'
Bob Dylan

Round 5 – December 19th 2015

Imagine standing on an aeroplane's wings as it flies at thirty thousand feet. Now imagine yourself standing on said aeroplane, this time with a golf club in your hand, and being asked to strike a golf ball into the 200mph headwind. There you have an accurate description of today's playing conditions in round five of our winter league journey. A six club wind buffeting us from pillar to post, balls oscillating on the greens, tree branches flying through the air, flagsticks breaking in two, the netting around the 3rd tee uprooted and blown onto the train tracks, the wind strong enough to blow your hair off never mind your hat. Mercifully there was no rain but the wind itself deemed the course virtually unplayable. Those that completed their rounds have been invited to Buckingham Palace to receive honorary knighthoods.

So it was in a veritable hurricane that the Russon/Douglas combo notched a very creditable 67 and for once, I'm prepared to concede that Douglas was the main man, standing up to the howling winds with a heroic back nine culminating in a miracle birdie on 18. It all started though with former Stonehaven club champion, Keith Douglas, suffering the ignominy of a second shot from the humps on the 1st having topped his drive. Crap footballers shouldn't wear pink boots, neither should golf club duffers play in bright orange Rickie Fowler breeks, but Douglas did. A retrospective stripping of Keith's championship titles seems rightful although he did redeem himself in spectacular style, knocking his second shot to twenty feet and draining the putt. A succession of pars followed, as did random chases across fairways in pursuit of tumbling golf caps, headcovers and trolleys. It was like a scene from the Benny Hill Show and I lost count of how often my backswing was serenaded by the sound of my carry bag crashing to the floor. For those who know the course, check out some of these club selections on the back nine; 14th – rescue, 15th – rescue, and on the last hole Keith nailed a full-on driver to be pin high for his birdie, that's a driver on a 172 yard par 3. Conditions were brutal.

We reached the sanctuary of the clubhouse to be greeted by a dozen older members wearing John Daly slacks and Christmas jumpers, about to embark on their festive shindig. If their all dayer in town was anywhere near as wild as our eighteen holes I'd be reading about it in the Sunday papers.

CHAPTER ELEVEN

'I'll never make that mistake again'
The Smiths

The local newspaper carried the following article at the end of December...

Rumours abound that the winter league partnership of Russon and Douglas will not make it into 2016. The relationship has been a tempestuous one from the outset but recent developments suggest the final nail has been hammered into the coffin. We asked Russon for his version of events.

'Douglas has been a difficult partner from the very beginning. A player of my calibre needs someone he can trust, a person of integrity, a partner to be relied upon for support and motivation, but from the outset the bloke has acted like a cretin. He complains that I don't replace flagsticks, grumbles that I don't complete the scorecard, runs me over with his remote controlled golf trolley and breaks wind in my backswing. I've had a quiet word with him but his behaviour shows no sign of improvement. I was close to throwing in the towel when he abandoned our fixture a few weeks ago in order to attend the Klitchko v Fury fight in Dusseldorf instead, and take a tour of the Becks Bier factory. What kind of commitment is that when your co-player dedicates his time to alcohol and international sport rather than playing eighteen holes on a freezing morning in Stoney? In the rain.

Douglas had been pleading throughout the Autumn for someone to partner him in the winter league. One member after another declined his advances, they were too polite to tell him to his face, but I'd heard through the grapevine that his halitosis had turned most of them away. Rumour had it that he could fell a horse from twenty paces, but I like to do my bit for the community, so agreed to partner him in the winter league. I took pity on him yet have been rewarded by petulance, poor golf and a succession of petty incidents until this week came the final straw.

He'd promised some blokes he worked with that he'd take them for a Christmas jolly to the bowling alley at Codonas in Aberdeen. He dropped this into conversation during our last round, I waited patiently for an invite, it wasn't forthcoming. Nevertheless, rather than take the huff, I graciously offered to drive his entourage from Stonehaven to Aberdeen since my car accommodates seven. This would save him money on taxi fares. He accepted my kind offer and the time was set for me to collect them from Troupers at 12.30 that coming Wednesday. My PA duly shuffled my diary, rearranging appointments with customers and colleagues (I have a very demanding senior executive position, my time is precious). Out of the kindness of my heart I allowed two hours from a tight schedule to ferry Keith and his herberts into town. You can imagine my disgust therefore when I arrived in Stonehaven to learn that they'd all piled into taxis and skidaddled. I telephoned Keith to voice my displeasure, the following is an account of the conversation".

'Keith? It's Alex. Where are you?'

'In a taxi, just passing Portlethen.'

'I said I'd take you all in.'

'Aye, but you didnae turn up.'

'Didn't turn up? I'm stood outside Troupers now.'

' I said 12.15'

'No you didn't, you said 12,30.'

" Aye but I texted this morn tae change it".

'I didn't get a text.'

'How nae? I sent it at 10.'

We then established that he'd sent it to the wrong number

'I told you I'd be here and I am here.'

'Aye well, I'm nae'

'Yes I've established that you tosser'

'Up yours Russon'

'Up yours yourself Douglas.'

*'Just f*ck off'*

*'No you f*ck off'*

*'Come here and say that you pr*ck'*

*'Tell the driver to stop and I f*cking will'.*

'Aye, you and who's army?'

...and so it continued, the conversation degenerating into personal insult without resolution. There I stood in my three piece suit, car engine running, waiting to take a collection of downbeats into town only to be stood up,

let down and abused for my trouble. There you have my winter league partner ladies and gentlemen, as trustworthy as a chocolate fireguard. I'm not one for violence but in Douglas's case it's crystal clear that the only language he understands is a good hiding. I know a couple of lads at a boozer I used to frequent in Walsall, I'll get them on the case. But don't report that bit'.

We understand the duo's respective management teams have organised peace talks with a view to fulfilling their winter league fixtures. The likelihood of a happy outcome is slim, not least because Douglas can't be trusted to arrive at the meeting on time, if at all. Time will tell, but as we stand today, the Stonehaven Golf Club Winter League trophy may be spared a terminal rusting by Keith Douglas's reputed bison breath.

CHAPTER TWELVE

'My little empire is as good as it can get'
Manic Street Preachers

A return to golf after a sustained break can go one of two ways, you either play like a demon or stink the course out. I usually play quite well after a rest, my head free of the paralysis of analysis that otherwise blights my golf, I just stand up to the ball and hit it. Cluttering of the mind is the bane of any golfer's life, thoughts crowd your head during the backswing and you're a shivering wreck by the time your club reaches the ball. A break from the game frees you of these fears, it gives you a blank slate, liberates you from the energy sapping thoughts of swing mechanics. Well for the front nine at least.

Equally disconcerting after a long lay off is the first tee terror when playing before a sizeable audience. He won't thank me for broadcasting this, but there was never a better example than my brother Stuart's meltdown at a plush corporate golf day in Nottinghamshire some years ago. Our fourball teed off in full view of dozens of golfers milling around the front of the clubhouse. Stu decided a 5-iron would be appropriate and, without so much as a practice swing, addressed his golf ball. His face set in stone, eyes on stalks, stricken with apprehension, he began the backswing and in a grotesque movement lasting a millisecond, completed less than a quarter of it before lurching at the ball in blind panic. His shoulders stiffened, his knees dipped and he delivered the fresh air shot to end all fresh air shots, his clubhead swishing the air a clear six inches above the ball. Playing partners coughed, Stuart gulped, it was an X-rated horror show.

And so to today, a full four weeks after our last game, round six of the winter league, an opportunity to play with freedom and no fear. It was with a degree of excitement then that I cleaned my clubs, polished my shoes, even washed my ball pocket. I had the demeanour of a child awaking on Christmas Day, full of expectation. Imagine my disappointment then when at the eleventh hour, my winter league partner cried off citing fatigue due to a late night bout of poker in Dundee. As excuses go, 'lame' doesn't even cover it. I suppose I should be grateful for the twelve hour notice of his absence but given I was notified by text in the dead of night, I was asleep for eight of those hours.

I shouldn't be surprised, he has form, having stood me up only last month when I'd had the good grace to offer him a lift to Aberdeen. Once again Douglas's behaviour proves itself to be beyond the pale and leaves me questioning the wisdom of having partnered this oaf in the winter league pairs. It comes to a pretty pass when the man you've been carrying through the winter league competition has the brass neck to cry off just as you pull into the club car park. Perhaps with his poker winnings he can buy himself a mirror and take a long hard look at himself.

*　　*　　*

Ahead of Stonehaven Golf Club's AGM, I took the trouble to propose a range of initiatives which I felt would enormously benefit the club's constitution. My ten point plan would revolutionise golf in Stonehaven and generate new levels of membership not seen since Tom Watson was rumoured to have bought the house behind the tenth.

To older members, some of these proposals may have appeared over ambitious, however I felt we mustn't fall foul of retrograde intransigence. Progress requires bravery and the committee needed to embrace change, put their best foot forward and grasp the future with both hands. Homer Simpson once said 'You don't win friends with salad,' similarly golf clubs don't win new members with old ideas. I therefore urged the committee to do their duty by rocking up in a few weeks time and approve the following forward thinking amendments.

1. Mulligans

The *mulligan* is a unique scoring mechanism which, while popular in bounce game circles, has never made it into the official R&A rulebook. Referred to by some as 'cheating', it's a once per round chance to reload, without penalty, having slashed a ball out of bounds or topped it into the undergrowth. It presents a welcome opportunity for despondent golfers to erase a howler from both memory and scorecard, proceeding as if it never happened, the two stroke penalty expunged from the record. In a radical departure from the somewhat archaic scoring system, the proposed Stoney mulligan will afford players the chance of atonement, the opportunity to dust themselves down and start again without penalty.

2. The Humps

There are few more pitiful sights at Stonehaven Golf Club than someone failing to reach the humps on the 1st hole. Situated barely one hundred yards in front of the tee, the humps decorate rather than protect the fairway and there's simply no excuse for one's ball to do anything other than sail over them.

As a youngster taking your first steps in the game, it is forgivable for your ball to fall short of the humps. As a grown man however, it is nothing but a public disgrace. I am therefore advocating that players who fail to place their opening drives beyond the humps must play their second shots with their trousers around their ankles. Such a policy will encourage members to improve their driving and as a consequence, the club will develop quality golfers rather than the shameful duffers we tolerate today.

A portable vanity shield will be kept between the practice green and the cemetery should any member have 'gone commando' and require a pair of Y-fronts for the purpose of playing their second shot. A selection of under garments will be available. On no account may members bare their backsides on the first hole fairway, or worse, reveal their furniture in full view of the clubhouse. We boast a vibrant Ladies section and have no desire to reverse this happy position. We cannot risk mass resignations because some old boy forgets to put his long johns on of a morning, duffs his drive beneath the clubhouse window and plays his second shot while revealing his meat and two veg.

Further penalties will be introduced should members repeat the offence. If a player on two consecutive occasions fails to reach the humps from the first tee, he must complete the hole in nothing but a leopard-skin thong and should the offence be repeated a third time, the entire eighteen holes must be completed in a luminous green mankini.

3. Championship Rules

I propose the following changes to the club championship entry criteria.

a) Entrants must be born between 28th August 1969 and 30th August 1969, not inclusive (ie. they must have been born only on the day in the middle).

b) Participants must have been born in the West Midlands.

c) And support Aston Villa

While this may narrow the field down somewhat, it throws the tournament wide open to players who don't carry the surname 'Irvine'. It's about time the trophy engraver was offered some variety, he's been inscribing the same names for years. It would also represent a well deserved gesture to one of the giants of Stonehaven Golf Club's history, a humble gentleman who selflessly followed his junior championship victory as a 16 year old with a return to his Birmingham roots, rather than dominate the golfing scene in Stonehaven. There's little doubt that this individual would have become a multiple winner of the club's flagship event had he remained in Stoney (in the event however he went to Birmingham Polytechnic, started drinking and didn't pick up a golf club for another nineteen years, but that's another story).

Further amendments to the club championship rules will be...

1)   Tournament reduced from 72 holes to 3 holes (Bruce's Corner ie. 1st, 2nd, 18th)

2)   Honorary lifetime membership awarded to the winner.

4.   7th Green Plaque

Stonehaven Golf Club prides itself on the upholding of golf's honourable traditions. Quite apart from obeying the edicts of the Royal & Ancient Rulebook, our members diligently protect the unwritten laws of etiquette that are synonymous with the sport. Except for one member; Keith Douglas, who's tawdry gamesmanship is well known. Amongst his 'attributes' are coughing in your backswing and walking on your line, to name but two. However, the tide turned, if only for a moment earlier this year, and to mark this chivalrous incident I'm proposing a plaque is erected in his honour alongside the 7th green.

We were playing a bounce game after work, 50p was at stake and I was six up after six before knocking my tee shot on the 7th to six inches while Douglas ferreted around his bag looking for a fresh ball having put two out of bounds already, despite perfect conditions. A few minutes later, as he retrieved his ball from the hole following a quintuple bogey eight, he grudgingly mumbled 'ye can huv 'at een' as I addressed my six inch tap-in. This represented the first putt he'd conceded since playing crazy golf with his father while on a Spanish holiday in the 1970s. As a testament to this event, a plaque will be erected (at Keith's expense) to provide encouragement to the junior members of the club that it's never too late for a golfer to change their ways and behave appropriately on a golf course. It doesn't matter how reprehensible your on course behaviour may have been for a sustained period of time, there is always the opportunity to atone. (Sadly I must report that Douglas followed this benevolent concession by stomping off the course having lost the match at the 10th before letting down my tyres when he reached the car park).

5. 12th hole to become a par 5

Let's take a look at some statistics regards the 12th hole :

3   Number of years since I started playing the 12th

1,471   Approx number of times I've played the 12th

3   Number of times I've parred the 12th

5.46   My average score on the 12th

24   Number of times I've broken down and wept on the 12th

89   Number of balls I've pulled into the trees
        on the bleedin' 12th

238   Number of times I've dreamt of blowing up the 12th

The 12th is a pig of a hole, no question, and I hereby demand that it's changed to a par five without any lengthening whatsoever, in fact I'm advocating it's reduction in length by forty yards. In a recent survey there was a 100% backing for this proposal (admittedly only involving me and my brothers Stu and Chris, for whom I voted by proxy) and you can't argue with bald facts like that.

In almost fifteen hundred attempts I've hit the green in regulation twice, both times three putting for bogey through pure shock. My three pars were the result of two chip-ins and a conceded twenty footer when a matchplay opponent had already racked up an eight. It's the only hole on the course I've never birdied and I'm fed up trying. Turn it into a par five pronto and get the course's standard scratch upped to 67.

6. Fill in the gully

My great Uncle Eric (Soutar) was a member of Stonehaven Golf Club for several years, during this time he was only once spotted playing the gully outside of a competitive round. He had zero appetite for the yomp down the path from the 13th tee and back again. It used to miff me mightily when I'd be on a good score after twelve holes only to end up playing the field twice because Eric wouldn't play the gully. Now that I'm no longer a whipper snapper, and instead a forty something with a bad back, I'm beginning to understand his stubborn reticence all those years ago. If records were produced detailing the least played holes on the course, the gully would come top by a mile. How many of us walk from the field or the 8th directly to the 16th tee instead of getting out the tie ropes and crampons?

I therefore propose that the gully is flattened and Aberdeenshire Council contracted to fill it in with ten thousand tonnes of landfill before turfing it to create a perfectly flat 13th, 14th and 15th. This initiative will be funded by the council themselves since they'd be placing their waste on the club's property and we'd be saving them money given their hospitals wouldn't need to deal with sporadic heart attacks induced by wheezing pensioners hauling their trolleys up the 13th. In addition, the club will benefit from the extra years of subscription fees given the gully redesign would extend member's lives by a couple of years minimum. I ain't stupid, I've costed this thing out and it makes absolute sense.

As a secondary proposal, were the committee so short sighted as to reject the gully landfill idea, I suggest we agree terms with a local taxi company to provide lifts across the gully at reduced fares, a fiver seems sensible. Taxi companies can provide lifts directly from the 15th green to the clubhouse for anyone NR'ing. 10% of this fare will be donated to the club to cover wear and tear of the path alongside the railway line and 10% towards the Alex Russon Trust Fund in respect of royalty payments for having come up with the idea to start with.

7. Revised stroke index

Who among us understands golf course stroke indexes? There appears to be no rhyme or reason to their selection. Should they be weighted regarding a hole's length rather than level of difficulty? Not in my estimation, but increasingly this seems to be the yardstick. Thankfully, one of SGC's many attributes is the sensible manner in which the stroke indexes are calculated, rather than automatically awarding high numbers to par threes, the club sensibly attributes stroke indexes according to difficulty and this is to be commended. Regrettably however, such prudence only applies to the first twelve holes and then all hell breaks loose, common sense being thrown to the wolves as four of the final six holes are given basket case indexes. Whoever selected the stroke indexes for the 13th, 14th, 15th and 17th needs a good talking to, they're so far off the mark as to be on another planet. Did the selectors ever play the gully or were they put off by the long walk? I can only surmise they spent their time picking numbers out of a hat while indulging in some clubhouse hospitality of the liquid kind.

The 13th for example, carries a stroke index of seven yet I've known players be put on suicide watch after scoring more than par here, it ought to be stroke index 19. The very next hole, a tricky, blind par three, is ludicrously deemed the sixth easiest hole on the course when in truth players dance a conga to the next tee if they share pars. But the piece de resistance, the glaring floater on the surface of flushed bog water, is the 15th hole being considered the third hardest hole on the course. This is insanity. Dame Edna Everidge in full ball gown and heels could par the 15th, left handed, blindfolded with a haversack upon her back. It's so straightforward that my father has notched a hole-in-one on it and believe me when I say he ain't no Tiger Woods. Granted, a facing wind has you going up a club or two but nine times out of ten it's a flick and a couple of putts, to award it stroke index three is preposterous.

Then we come to the 17th, the peskiest hole on the course, the closest I've come to tears outside of childbirth (attending not delivering). It's been my scorecard shredder more times than I care to remember, the green as welcoming as my mother-in-law, its sloped approach sending your ball scurrying down the hill towards the 3rd tee. A couple of fluffed chips later, as you attempt the parachute shot onto the green, and you're stomping off with a seven on your card. Despite this, the stroke index of five is pure comedy and must be amended forthwith. I confess my travails on this hole are purely due to my mindset, my stinking thinking, I just can't stand the hole, it's not difficult it's just my bogey hole, everybody has them. If you get a good drive away you can be putting for eagle, how in heaven's name it can be classed as the fifth most difficult is beyond me.

I therefore announce that 2016 will usher in a full review of the club's stroke indexes with members being balloted before a final decision is reached. In fact scrub that, the ballot's already been held and here are the results, I give you the new stroke indexes for Stonehaven Golf Club (former ones in brackets) –

1st 14	(12)	10th 9	(9)
2nd 2	(4)	11th 17	(17)
3rd 12	(14)	12th 1	(1)
4th 3	(8)	13th 19	(7)
5th 7	(2)	14th 6	(13)
6th 11	(16)	15th 10	(3)
7th 8	(10)	16th 15	(15)
8th 18	(18)	17th 13	(5)
9th 4	(6)	18th 5	(11)

8. Stonehaven GC twinning

Stonehaven Golf Club's announcement that it was 'twinning' with Letham Grange Golf Club left me with mixed emotions. While I looked forward to enjoying Letham at the earliest opportunity, I must confess to bittersweet feelings over the arrangement.

Unbeknown to the SGC committee, I'd been involved in hush hush negotiations with another golf club regarding a similar arrangement until the Letham announcement put the kybosh on it. A confidentiality clause prevents me from naming the club in question, but I am at liberty to reveal it was an inner city Birmingham location and negotiations had reached an advanced stage. Only a few loose ends remained and while congratulating Letham Grange on the deal struck, I can't help but wonder what might have been had the last few issues been resolved by their Birmingham counterparts, namely :-

1. Removal of the last eight dozen empty beer cans from the back nine.

2. Return to Asda of all shopping trolleys floating in the canal adjacent to the 7th fairway.

3. Eviction of the four winos who've set up camp in the deep bushes by the 4th.

4. Repair of quad bike tracks left on the 12th green following last week's police chase from the local jewellers.

5. Dismissal of the club secretary for supporting Birmingham City.

6. Installation of a thirty foot security fence alongside the 3rd hole to protect players from a stoning by homeward bound school kids.

7. Citizen's arrest of the golf ball thieves brazenly marching from the bushes to lift balls from the 4th green (see no3 above).

8. Appointment of car park security guard to ensure players no longer return to their vehicles to find them on bricks.

The committee rather jumped the gun when approving the Letham Grange initiative. Nevertheless, it is to be applauded that they nominated a club that doesn't count Jasper Carrot amongst its membership.

9. Discipline

'Spare the rod, spoil the child' so the saying goes. While not advocating corporal punishment for the non-repair of divots, I feel standards of golfing behaviour mustn't be allowed to degenerate. I therefore propose a suite of measures that will ensure SGC safeguards its reputation in North Eastern golfing circles.

- Prohibition of ankle bangers. Senior members will no longer be permitted to wear their twenty year old breeks at half mast.

- 6 month ban for the playing of Penfold Commandos or Dunlop 65s

- Golfers taking fresh air shots will be reported to the police

- Players scoring over 100 will be placed into stocks on the practice putting green and pelted with rotten fruit

- Anyone taking four putts on one hole will be suspended

- The following sayings are now banned from putting greens; you dropped your lipstick, dead sheep, does your husband play?

- Failure to clear the gully from the 13th tee will require the culprit to reload wearing a bell encrusted jester's hat

- Banning of tee pegs attached to mini pom poms

- Two consecutive shanks will attract a lifetime ban

The introduction of these measures can only enhance the performance of players and the reputation of the club. We cannot expect to be taken seriously when ill attired players are swishing fresh air shots over the top of Penfold Commandos perched on tees attached to bright yellow pom poms.

10. It's A Knockout

Remember *It's A Knockout*, that wacky game show in the 70s/80s? The less said about its presenter the better but the concept of the show was a good one. The best bit was when a team played their joker to win double points and I've decided SGC will adopt this idea in Stableford competitions.

From the beginning of the summer season, each player will nominate a hole on the front and back nine upon which they'll play their joker. Double points will be awarded on these holes, for example, a par will earn four points and not two. But you need to get wise with it, there's no point nominating the 9th if that's the hole upon which you regularly falter, double zilch is still zilch. Better to choose a hole upon which you score well, if that's not stating the bleeding obvious. Players cannot nominate the holes retrospectively and must make clear before their round commences which holes will benefit from double bubble.

And in a cheeky twist to encourage a level playing field, those with handicaps below six will have a reverse joker whereby the number of *strokes* they play on the nominated hole are doubled, not their points tally. For instance, if they show off with a three on the first this is doubled to six which equals a blob. Indeed they'd need to eagle the first to score any points at all. This may appear a touch harsh but will bring the swaggerers down to size and how beautiful will it be, when their birdies count for naught on the very same hole a high handicapped player's birdie earns them six points! Sweet.

And it is with this tenth and final initiative that I conclude my proposed amendments to the Stonehaven Golf Club constitution. Happy golfing everyone, letters of appreciation for my inspirational blueprint can be addressed to the club secretary.

_____

CHAPTER THIRTEEN

'It's too late for apologies and falling at your feet'
Kings Of Leon

In the absence of a golf report (course closed due to snow), I'll share a letter with you which I received from a solicitor this week.

Dear Mr Russon

It has been brought to our attention by our client, K Douglas Esq of Stonehaven, that you have been publishing libellous material about him. Upon examination of your blog 'Stoney Baloney', we are in full agreement with our client and hereby demand action is taken before legal proceedings are sought. We have been instructed to act in the strongest possible terms and, if you'll pardon the vulgarity, been requested, in our client's words, to 'take you to the fu#*ing cleaners.' We therefore insist that you publish a full retraction of your slanderous comments, issue a comprehensive apology and allow our client the right of reply on your tiresome blog. If action is not taken within 7 days, we have been instructed by our client to sue you for every penny you've got and pursue you to the ends of the earth in this regard.

We await your response.

Yours sincerely

B. Hind Barrs Solicitors

As you can imagine, it was quite a shock to receive this letter, and not a little unsettling. My children have subsequently experienced nightmares believing I'm going to prison, and my wife has threatened to leave me. However, if my winter league partner is without sufficient honour to deal with this face to face, I have no choice but to fall on my sword and carry out the instructions given by his solicitor. Moreover, if I'm to retain any hope of seizing the winter league trophy I'll need to fulfil the remaining fixtures alongside Douglas so I'd best keep him sweet. I therefore issue the following response *'in all sincerity'* and confirm that the accusations I made against him were indeed *'a figment of my imagination'*.

> *Dear Keith*
>
> *I write to confirm that you did not thieve money from my golf bag while I was putting out on the 7th green (even though you were the only person within 500 yards). I also retract the suggestion that I carry you around the course while you contribute nothing towards our team effort (please return the bill submitted to you by my back physio). In addition, I confirm you do not have poor etiquette, shocking dress sense, halitosis, bad flatulence or a potty mouth. You did not stand me up when I kindly arrived to collect you for a lift into Aberdeen before Christmas, you don't belch in my backswing and at no time have you let my tyres down in the club car park.*
>
> *I hope this 'heartfelt' apology is satisfactory to you and that you will continue with our partnership for the*

remainder of the winter league. You are indeed a fine upstanding pillar of the community, a man of integrity and it is my great fortune that you stooped low enough to accept me as your partner (even if everybody else had turned you down flat). I'm sorry for any distress I may have caused, rest assured there will be no repeat of any inaccurate criticism I have levelled against you.

I look forward with relish to our reunion next Saturday on the 1st tee. Upon arrival, please don't be distracted by the welcoming committee of black suited bouncers from the boozer I drank in when residing in inner city Birmingham. Furthermore, do not be disturbed by their surly manner or the vast array of instruments of torture which they're likely to exhibit. Your safety is, I guarantee, assured. In closing, I also apologise for the discovery of a horse's head in your scratcher this morning, I accidentally misplaced it when driving home from work.

Yours without contempt and in friendship alone

Alex Russon

I then received another letter from Douglas's solicitor, this time insisting that I publish, upon my blog, his client's legal right of reply and that it must occupy the same amount of space as my 'libellous' assertions. Douglas had penned this reply himself, quite an achievement for an illiterate imbecile such as him, in fact I had no doubt it had been ghost written. Here it is, I'll leave you to decide whether to believe a single word.

Keith Douglas Right To Reply

I first met Russon in 1983. He pitched up at Stonehaven Golf Club wearing burgundy drainpipes and a Fred Perry, I remember thinking 'what an arse' and, over forthcoming years, was proved right.

I played golf with him because nobody else would, I took pity on him. We'd play through the summer holidays, the winner getting a golf ball from the other's bag, but it was futile me winning, he only kept Dunlops. I used to drop them straight onto the floor and smash them over the cliff.

After a while I got bored beating him at golf, so I'd fleece him at cards instead. We'd sit in the clubhouse playing three card brag and I'd clean him out of his dinner money. Then we switched to snooker and finally darts until he refused to remove his darts from the board after fluking a 180. I expect they're still in the board to this day the fat show off.

He'd moved up from Birmingham and would drone on about Aston Villa. I couldn't give a sh*t about English football, Gary Shaw or Villa Park, it was of no interest to me. Neither was his music, he played Depeche Mode endlessly, I couldn't stand them, I still can't. His dress sense hasn't improved over time, he's still wearing the same crap gear today, his golf trousers doubling up as his 'goin' out' breeks, I expect he goes to bed in them, the tink.

Finally, in 1986, he buggered off back to Birmingham. I thought I'd heard the last of him but out of the blue, thirty years later, he's back again, hanging around like a bad smell. I never learn and gave in to his pleading for a winter league partner, big mistake. He still bangs on about Aston Villa, they're even crapper now than they were then, and so is his golf. He writes the biggest heap of junk on that flaming blog of his, pretending he's the main man when the truth is he contributes nothing. He can't chip, can't putt and is a complete bottler, when he does scrape the odd par I never hear the end of it. And if I hear him brag one more time that he was Junior Champion in '86 I'll brain him. I was club champion in 2000 and 2006 but don't feel the need to remind him on every tee.

This winter league has been an eye opener. It's unrealistic to expect a completely even spread of the workload between us but even 70/30 would be a luxury where Russon's concerned. I estimate he's contributed no more than 10% of the scores we've recorded, the rest has been down to me. He's like Bez from The Happy Mondays, bringing nothing but a silly grin and a crap haircut. He offers nothing. He's not even a cheerleader. Absolutely hopeless. He's all mouth and no trousers and I go on record in saying the day he returned to Stoney was the worst day of my life. Bog off back to Birmingham you lightweight and take your blog with you.

CHAPTER FOURTEEN

'Aint he cool, no he aint'
The Specials

Round 6 – February 6th 2016

It's been a triumphant week for my winter league partner, Keith Douglas. First, he got his cheapies becoming an internet sensation with an online video going viral and second, he came to the party in round six of our winter league partnership.

First the online stardom. He recorded a nine second video which achieved a remarkable quarter of a million hits in two days. Of the following three situations, two are false and one is correct, which do you reckon his video footage depicted?

1.   Crossing an old lady over the road?

2.   The touching moment when a young child is reunited with his father returning from an armed forces' foreign posting?

3.   Mercilessly mocking the Celtic management team as they skulk back to the dressing room having lost to Aberdeen?

Correct. His 'Nelson off The Simpsons' style 'ha ha' ridiculing of John Collins & Ronnie Daeila proved such a hit that it was seen by hundreds of thousands, some of whom were Celtic supporters ready to tear him to shreds. I'd have held their coats.

As for Keith's second triumph of the week, he finally turned in a performance at Stonehaven Golf Club in our winter league partnership. It was pretty frosty when we met and I don't mean the weather, our exchange of solicitor's letters had done nothing to soften an atmosphere that was already crackling with animosity. When we alighted at the golf club Douglas didn't receive me warmly, I was standing beneath the clubhouse window speaking to Barry McGilvary when his royal knobness appeared at the window, looked in my direction and drew an index finger across his throat. He may have had an itchy neck but I suspect not. He could look forward to another letter from my brief following that unprovoked gesture.

'You deserve a medal for playing the entire winter league with that pillock,' said Barry, 'he really is an insufferable arsehole, hats off to you for putting up with golf's biggest waster since Maurice Flitcroft, you have my sympathy.' Barry's words not mine, but I can only concur.

Credit, however, where it's due, Douglas today putting aside the distraction of our legal disagreement to play eighteen holes of competent golf. This was our sixth round and while his contribution had until this point been paltry, he finally came to the party with birdies on 1, 10 and 17, while parring most of the other holes. For my part, I had an uncharacteristic off-day due to jogger's nipple suffered during my morning run. Some might say Douglas's round of 68 wasn't all that impressive given we were playing the course at its most benign, and I must concede there is truth in that suggestion. We were indeed playing a foreshortened winter course, virtually every par four was driveable with a half decent contact, the par threes demanded no more than a flick with a pitching wedge, the holes on the temporary greens were cut to the size of hula hoops and preferred lies offered the chance to tee the ball up on a hand picked tuft of grass every time you missed the fairway. It may seem churlish to suggest that anyone capable of holding a golf club the right way round could have broken 70, but it ain't far from the truth. Nevertheless, I shouldn't belittle Keith's achievement, I'll get another missive from his brief otherwise, so would like to congratulate him on a well executed round of golf, despite the course lying on its proverbial back waiting for its tummy to be tickled.

CHAPTER FIFTEEN

'You've got a lot of nerve to say you are my friend'
Bob Dylan

Here's a taster of the type of nonsense I had to put up with week after week. Befriend Douglas on Facebook at your peril.

Keith Douglas Your a Clown Russon!!!!!!
Like · Reply · 1 · 8 February at 17:02

Alex Russon See you in court Douglas
Like · Reply · 1 · 8 February at 18:42

Keith Douglas You will that!!!!!!!
Like · Reply · 1 · 8 February at 18:43

Alex Russon You'll need a better brief than you have a tailor you scruffbag
Like · Reply · 1 · 8 February at 18:49

Keith Douglas Another insult!!!! Keep it up!!!!!!
Like · Reply · 1 · 8 February at 19:13

Alex Russon Well since you insist, your feet stink.
Like · Reply · 1 · 8 February at 19:44

Barry Mcgillivray Superb.havnt laughed so much in ages
Like · Reply · 1 · 8 February at 20:31

Keith Douglas Away and throw s""the at yourself you p""ck
Like · Reply · 8 February at 21:50

Keith Douglas All gone quite Russon! Not like it back at you????
Like · Reply · 9 February at 20:39

Alex Russon I thought you were addressing Barry?
Like · Reply · 9 February at 21:10

Keith Douglas Don't have a problem with him!
Like · Reply · 9 February at 21:38

Alex Russon Are you startin' like?

Keith Douglas I'll finish it!!!!!!
Like · Reply · 9 February at 23:42

Alex Russon You reckon?You're hard as my first sh#te and that was a skitter.
Like · Reply · 10 February at 06:54

Keith Douglas You are just one big skitter!
Like · Reply · 10 February at 12:11

Alex Russon One big skitter who can put a 3 wood 30 yards past your driver any day of the week.
Like · Reply · 10 February at 17:59

Keith Douglas Aye and walk off with a double bogey you tit! Can't pitch or put to save your sad life!
Like · Reply · 10 February at 18:35

Alex Russon my A game comes in the summer, don't waste it in the winter. You'll see Douglas.
Like · Reply · 10 February at 18:40

Keith Douglas You'll be lucky if you see the summer! Especially at SGC
Like · Reply · 10 February at 18:41

Alex Russon Summer = my dazzling birdie blitz time. Buy some sunglasses.
Like · Reply · 10 February at 19:33

Keith Douglas Buy some lessons you idiot!
Like · Reply · 10 February at 19:41

Alex Russon No need. Form is temporary, class is permanent.
Like · Reply · 10 February at 19:43

Keith Douglas Lol clown

Alex Russon taks een tae ken een min
Like · Reply · 10 February at 20:04

Keith Douglas And stop speaking like that! You plank
Like · Reply · 10 February at 20:10

Alex Russon me a plank? if your brains were dynamite you couldn't blow your hat off Douglas.
Like · Reply · 10 February at 21:04

Keith Douglas Least I have a brain!
Like · Reply · 1 · 10 February at 21:14

Alex Russon try using it then you gormless oaf
Like · Reply · 1 · 10 February at 21:15

Keith Douglas I will when I choose a real partner next year!
Like · Reply · 10 February at 21:40

Alex Russon some other mug to replace flagsticks and listen to your guff all the way round, feel free
Like · Reply · 10 February at 21:41

Keith Douglas You've put 3 flags in in 6 rounds and marked the card twice! Which I suppose is more than the total holes you contribute per round you hacking muppet!!!!!

Alex Russon Up yours. I weigh in plenty.
Like · Reply · 10 February at 21:57

Keith Douglas Yeah you need go on a diet you fat f**k!!!!
Like · Reply · 10 February at 22:08

Alex Russon You call me fat! You're carrying more timber than the forestry commission you grotesque porker.
Like · Reply · 11 February at 09:54 · Edited

Keith Douglas Keep going Russon! You'll be getting sent back to where you come from at this rate! And THEY DONT WANT YOU EITHER! P"""k!!!!!!
Like · Reply · 11 February at 13:18

Alex Russon Not before I've given you a good hiding Douglas. Just been up the club and seen WL scores, we're trailing in other folk's wake thanks to your ineptitude.
Like · Reply · 11 February at 15:31

Keith Douglas Russon you've done F""k all so far so shut your F""king face before I knock you into next week! What a TIT!!!!
Like · Reply · 11 February at 15:38

Alex Russon You appear to be overlooking my barrage of birdies in round 3 while you were trying to work out which end of the club to use.
Like · Reply · 11 February at 17:14

Keith Douglas Lol! The only barrage you've had is a barrage of abuse towards me! Closest you've been to a birdie was when you almost hit a seagull floating in the North Sea!

Alex Russon At least I can make it past the humps you donkey.
Like · Reply · 11 February at 18:09

Keith Douglas Least I'm SCOTTISH!!!!!!!!!!!! Get it right UP YA!!!!! B
Like · Reply · 11 February at 18:22

Alex Russon What's your nationality got to do with the price of cheese? You could be Swahili for all I care but you still couldn't make it past the humps.
Like · Reply · 11 February at 18:32

Keith DouglasConstruction Think you'll find I wasn't short of the humps you clown! As for you hitting 3 trains last week! Your a joke min!!!!!!

91

CHAPTER SIXTEEN

'What you did was so obscene'
The Charlatans

I'd never been to a physio before today, hells bells it's a bit previous isn't it? I ambled in complaining of back pain and she had me down to my underpants within five minutes. You mustn't blame the woman, I can't help being irresistible, but we could have exchanged pleasantries for a little longer first.

The sharpest pain was in my buttocks (there's a joke there but I'm too tired to work it out) so she lay me down, turned me over and worked on my right arse cheek, grinding in her elbow to locate the pain's epicentre. There's something disconcerting about a woman, to whom you've barely said hello, touching your arse. 'I'm freeing up the fibres matted in your bottom', she said. 'That's what I do when I change my son's nappy' I snorted. No, she didn't laugh either.

As I remained face down, she pushed her palms up and down my spine. 'Any pain yet?' she enquired. 'No," I lied. There was pain alright, but it was in my testicles as she shoved so hard on my coccyx that my rollocks were getting flattened against the bed beneath, but I was too embarrassed to tell her. Eventually, I returned to my feet, middle age spread tumbling over my elasticated underpants, my glory trussed up like coconuts in a hammock. Damn it, why didn't I wear something more flattering? Mercifully, she instructed me to put my feeble body back into a pair of breeks and a t-shirt. 'Same time next week?' she said. 'Fine' I grunted. I now had seven days to find myself a decent pair of Y-fronts.

*   *   *

My golf was poor last week. Duck hooks on the 9th and 10th threatened travellers on passing trains and a preposterous slice on the 16th cleared the railway track. Long irons were slapped, pitches muffed, it was a miserable performance opening the door for Douglas to ridicule me all the way round but then I'd become accustomed to his infantile behaviour over six tiresome rounds with the useless waster.

Wounded by his criticism, I was determined my next game would see a vast improvement, so booked another appointment with my doctor to address the worsening back pain that was causing my golf to suffer. The physio's recent efforts had done nothing positive, regrettably, so I was back at the quack's again, but to suggest this doctor's visit was harrowing would be an understatement.

I shuffled into his surgery giving him a description of my ailment, before handing over a letter addressed to him from the physio. Having peered over his spectacles to read the letter, he ushered me across to the examination table, explaining the letter had suggested other issues may be at play and this required investigation.

'It could be a kidney complaint or more likely a urinary problem,' he said, 'until we rule these or other causes out, it's difficult to diagnose. Drop your trousers and underpants below your knees please.'

'Pardon?!' I replied, somewhat taken aback.

'Breeks doon, airse oot, you won't feel a thing.'

'What are you going to do?', I was getting worried.

'A rectal examination, we need to check your prostate' he replied.

'Hold on, I've got a sore back, what's my backside got to do with it?'

'I've explained the situation Mr Russon, we're investigating all possibilities. I'll book you in for blood tests but first we need to check your prostate. Lie down on your side and face the wall.'

And before you could say 'Jack Robinson' or 'I want my Mummy', he'd plunged his middle finger deep into my back passage and was rummaging around as if searching for a lost set of keys in a car's glovebox. It wasn't painful and was over in seconds, but I have to confess it was somewhat disconcerting having another man part my butt cheeks and send a digit through my rusty sheriff's badge. I'd entered the room expecting the obligatory urine sample yet here was a veritable stranger seeking access to my inards via my chocolate starfish. It came as quite a surprise I can tell you.

We returned to our seats, in silence. He spoke about blood tests but I wasn't really listening, I was busy recreating a mental image of what had just transpired and worrying about the state of my ringpiece. Had I performed an adequate clean up operation last time I'd parked my breakfast or had my arse wept pungent matter over his finger? Thankfully he didn't appear too repulsed by the procedure but then again, he was hardly likely to share a description of his findings. We shook hands, mercifully he'd washed his, and parted company. It was all over in a flash but I returned to the car park muttering furiously under my breath. "I'll kill Douglas for this."

Yes I blame Douglas. It's all his miserable fault. Had he encouraged rather than chastised me last Saturday, offered words of support rather than criticism, I doubt I'd have felt the need to make another doctor's appointment, I'd have put my poor performance down to a bad day at the office and moved on. But since he'd gone to such lengths to demoralise me, I felt compelled to have my injury dealt with and to show him just how good a golfer I could be. The doctor's appointment, and subsequent anal examination, was all down to him.

He would pay for this and no mistake. Nobody facilitates the investigation of my marmite runway and gets away with it. If you're reading this Keith, and I don't want you to be unduly alarmed, I thought I'd share with you a summary of a recent article in *The Guardian* (that's a broadsheet newspaper with big words commentating on current affairs, not a comic such as those to which you're accustomed, telling the world about Cheryl Cole's latest squeeze). This article described the popularity of medieval re-enactments, groups of folk dressing up in medieval garb and providing staged productions so that people could better understand what life was like centuries ago. These re-enactments were very realistic and included accounts of various methods of torture meted out to criminals of the age. Amongst these punishments was the 'red hot poker', a particularly ghastly instrument, an iron spindle heated to an extremely high temperature and then inserted into the guilty party's bottom. The victim would suffer this invasion of his nethers a number of times until passing out with the pain before awaking to have it repeated all over again. And again. And again. Apparently, I was reading, the stage effects from these travelling Medieval drama groups can go missing and are *later found to have been stolen by members of the general public for nefarious personal use.*

Did you know Keith, as luck would have it, one of these re-enactments is scheduled for Stonehaven every year, on a date where there's a perpetual window in my diary. I suggest you keep this in mind because if you find yourself within a million miles of the area you just might find one of these instruments is heated until it's white hot, never mind red hot, and locates itself a significant distance up your ample backside until it's tip appears through your nostrils. This is not a threat, it is a promise.

CHAPTER SEVENTEEN

'The circus is in town'
Bob Dylan

Round 7 – February 13th 2016

You play in some pretty cold conditions during the winter league but this weekend was beyond Baltic. We were kitted out in hats, snoods, scarves, balaclavas and that's before we left the clubhouse. Try swinging a golf club when you're wearing enough layers to set up a chain of clothes shops. Still, it was dry and the sun was shining, be grateful for small mercies.

Keith and I were playing our seventh round of the winter league, this time alongside two senior members, Donald Gordon and Derek Freeland. I went to school with Donald's daughter, Tanya, back in the 80s and asked what she was doing these days. When he explained she was a lawyer in Edinburgh I left the conversation there, there's nothing worse than feeling inadequate. I switched the chat over to Derek only to discover he was the owner of a sizeable local business, so I packed in talking to him too. Ego bruised, I buried my hands into my pockets and walked on.

Your ten best scores are aggregated at the end of the league fixtures to decide upon qualification for the final. We're in the mix, our scores averaging better than par, but we needed to maintain momentum with a good round today and this we duly delivered (well I did, my partner playing second fiddle once again). We were conscious that a score of 66 or better was imperative, so when Keith muffed the first hole with a scruffy bogey it was important I stepped up to the plate with a solid par four, something I accomplished with aplomb. We grubbed along without any fireworks for the next three holes, until I took charge with a spectacular tap-in birdie on the 5th while Keith continued to contemplate his naval, I narrowly missed a birdie on the following hole too. I don't want to describe the entire round, there's nothing more tiresome than a golfer bragging about his performance, but suffice to say I took responsibility for our team's score while Keith weighed in only sporadically. He nudged in a birdie putt on 10 but that apart, wasn't at the races. I'm sad to say the atmosphere was once again pretty poor between us, indeed we almost came to blows on the 16th following an incident typifying his selfish attitude.

The 16th is a par five which I made mincemeat out of with a booming drive and medium iron to eight feet while Keith scrambled his way to the green in three shots. Miraculously however, Keith holed his birdie putt leaving me with a free hit at an eagle. Most partners would encourage and cajole their teammate, help them line the putt up and offer words of support. Not Keith, he mumbled something unrepeatable, trod on my line and as I began my backswing, returned his putter to his golf bag with enough noise to drown out a helicopter launch. This distraction was sufficient to put me off and miss the eagle attempt, Keith providing a soundtrack of bellowed laughter as my putt missed to the right. What a loser. I was strongly tempted to offer him out there and then but thought better of it, Donald and Derek didn't need to see blood on the dancefloor, but if he does it again I'll break his bleedin' nose.

The round ended with a par, mine, naturally, which achieved our targeted total of 66. There are three rounds to go and, provided we don't knock each other's blocks off, we hope to qualify. The good news for Messrs Gordon & Freeland was that their 18 holes with Keith ended right there, the bad news for them was that we were scheduled to accompany them again next weekend.

CHAPTER EIGHTEEN

*'In my life, why do I smile at people
who I'd much rather kick in the eye'*
The Smiths

Round 8 – February 21st 2016

I've given Keith some deserved stick on my blog lately and some had questioned whether we'd remain on speaking terms long enough to complete the tournament. I couldn't guarantee that, but for a split second today we found ourselves sharing a joke and Keith's brother, Jack, was on hand to record the event for posterity, taking a pleasant photograph with Skatie Shore in the background. I forget what the joke was now but our merriment lasted no more than seconds, once Douglas realised I'd given him the 'bunny ears' treatment when his brother took the photo, he lost control and offered to beat me up. So much for our reconciliation.

I rescued our meandering round today with a birdie on 17 after Keith had carelessly shoved his drive out of bounds. He looked on sheepishly while I holed a tricky six footer to cement our eighteen hole total of 65 keeping us well in the hunt for the final.

It could have been a different story, the round had begun spectacularly with Keith holing an eagle putt on the 1st after grubbing a thinner off the tee all the way to the winter green. After that however, it was merely a series of eventless, relentless pars. Once again I parred the entire gully, check the scorecard Douglas if you don't believe me, and Keith contributed his solitary birdie on the very short par five 16th. Steady, unspectacular golf was the order of the day and Jack's company ensured his brother and I didn't come to fisticuffs on the 7th when I threatened to use that unflattering photograph of him in this book. He made it crystal clear that were I to use said picture, it would be the last photograph my mobile phone ever took unless I found a way to retrieve the device from three foot up my backside. Charming.

So a 65 and one step closer to completing our ten rounds. It's quite possible Keith and I have only three more rounds of golf to share before the winter league draws to a close. I'd like to say it's been a pleasure... but ...

CHAPTER NINETEEN

'Don't send me no more letters no, not unless you mail them from desolation row'

Bob Dylan

Round 9 – February 27th 2016

Is it a bird? Is it a plane? No, it's Keith Douglas failing to reach the humps again. Today saw a classic faux pas by the hapless Douglas, you just couldn't make it up.

When I greeted him by the 1st tee, I was introduced to the solicitor he'd appointed in his libel case against me. Apparently the continued abuse of him on my blog had persuaded him to take matters further, to the sheriff court. The crux of his case appeared to be that I exaggerated his ineptitude and failed to give him sufficient credit for our team scores, all of which was patent nonsense which I had little doubt the judge would laugh out of court. Anyway, there he stood by the first tee, appraising his solicitor of latest developments, bleating on about my latest 'insulting' report in which I again called him out for being crap. He goes on to grumble about me claiming all the glory from our best rounds while blaming him for our bad ones, whining that he's nowhere near the rotten player that I describe him to be. Finally the moaning stops and he steps up to his opening tee shot, and what does he do? He duffs it fifty yards! Not only does his ball fail to reach the humps, it fails to get even halfway, the halfwit near on hits a fresh air shot! I looked over at his solicitor to find him scribbling what I can only surmise was a resignation letter having witnessed first hand that I'd been telling the truth all along. Lawyers want dead certs, this prospective client hadn't a leg to stand on, priceless. I couldn't contain myself and blurted out my thoughts before counting to ten;

'You shot yourself in the foot there Douglas and no mistake. No brief will get you out of this one you useless gimp. You're bang to rights son. In your face Douglas, in your face. If you had any sense you'd withdraw your threat of legal action before you make any more of a fool of yourself. No lawyer will take you seriously, save your money and buy some lessons instead chum.'

Turning now to the rest of the round, we scored a gross 63 which was highly commendable given we were on winter greens and the cold was intense. Our playing partners, Colin Polson and Martin McCoy, notched a nett 59 and were excellent company, they'll testify that I provided the lion's share of our scores once again with Keith playing no more than a supporting role, until a par at the last. I shone through despite being hampered by two injuries; a poorly finger following a disagreement with an Irn Bru bottle's screw top, and a bad back. I'd been to the physio again in the week, she's been trying to ease my back pain for a while now but has succeeded only in humiliating me so far. Week one she had me shivering in my smalls, week two she inadvertently flattened my testicles and week three was laughing at my arse.

'Your bottom isn't offering any support to your back when you go running', she said, 'you've got a jelly for a bottom, there's no muscle tone to your buttocks. They're meant to act as shock absorbers for the base of your spine but with you having such a weak bottom they do nothing.' she finished. The cheek. Shivering moobs, pancaked bollocks and a fat arse. What next? A swollen helmet? Cracked ringpiece? I've a good mind to sack her off.

Our 63 was the result of 15 pars and 3 birdies (10, 16, 17) with a number of clutch putts saving our bacon. I found myself having to shoulder the bulk of the burden, nervelessly sinking six footers on 2, 4, 7, 9 and 12. In addition I routinely parred the gully leaving Douglas to question whether he'd bother to even play it in future. Quite right too, that's six rounds straight that I've parred it now.

Things took a turn for the worse on the 16th fairway, adjacent to the 4th, as we waited to play our second shots. The three herberts on the 4th tee were peppering us with badly hooked drives and we were hopping about, like cats on a hot tin roof, to avoid them.

'It's a shame one of those didn't knock your f*cking teeth out Russon' said Keith.

I chortled, thinking he was joking, but turned to find his poker face staring me through. I glared back at his gormless mug, and like a pair of pre-fight heavyweight boxers, we held our stare, eyeballing one another, our noses virtually touching. Words were not exchanged for several seconds until Douglas broke the silence, his words seething through gritted teeth.

'The moment this competition is over Russon, I swear to you, I will see to it that you are ruined. Forever.'

'What are you talking about Douglas?'

'You think you're clever with that f*cking blog of yours, spouting a' that sh*te, yer winna be laughin when yer kids are visiting you in Peterheid.'

He wasn't messing, his words delivered with a chillingly sinister stare. 'I'll ruin you, just wait.'

CHAPTER TWENTY

'Look at all the people with their heads in their hands'
Eels

The next day, after much deliberation, I was forced to release the following statement to the world's media.

It is with great regret that I today announce my unavailability for the forthcoming Ryder Cup at Hazeltine, Minnesota. Rumours have been circulating that I would be an automatic wildcard pick however I hereby confirm that I will not be making myself available for selection. I have telephoned team captain, Darren Clarke, and would like to place on record my appreciation for the way he received this 'shattering news' (his words).

I'd like to take this opportunity to thank my fans for their continued support. My withdrawal has not been an easy decision but, given the circumstances, I believe it to be the right one. Family comes first and I've to take my daughter to choir practice on the Saturday, and my wife's car needs taking in for a service. Darren pleaded with me to play in the Sunday singles but I declined on the basis that team morale would be adversely affected were I to bump Rory off the anchor role. Besides, we go to the in-laws for a roast on Sundays.

In conclusion I'd like to reassure the Stonehaven Golf Club committee that I plan to honour, in full, my commitment to the 2016 schedule and as a gesture of gratitude for their continued support, will reduce my appearance fee for the New Year's Day Sair Heid competition by 10%[1]. (I will be available for autographs and selfies however these will be charged at the normal rate).

---

1 Provided I'm chauffeur driven to the course and given a massage in between the first and second nines.

CHAPTER TWENTY ONE

'Some local loser'
Bob Dylan

Thirty two teams entered The Winter League Scratch Pairs competition and as we entered the last knockings, eight were still in with a chance of qualifying for the final. A detailed explanation of the rules would have you losing the will to live, suffice to say the final would be contested by the four teams with the ten lowest accumulative scores. Let's just leave the accompanying rules and sub-rules for another day.

Miraculously, Keith Douglas and I were still in with a shout. Despite months of squabbling, name calling and regular exchanges of solicitor's letters, we remained a partnership and sat in fourth position with an average score of 66. The three leading partnerships were each averaging 64 and looked nailed on for qualification which left a straight fight between five other teams, ours included, with average scores ranging from 66-69. In truth, it was probably tatties,for the Arthur/Officer combo at 69 but who knew, they may yet shoot the lights out. It was definitely tatties for anyone scoring worse than an average of 69, great big hairy ones shaped like phallic symbols. Sadly, some partnerships had scored so poorly that 'tatties' doesn't cover it, an entire Aberdeenshire potato crop couldn't ably describe their chances and in one particular case the gross domestic output of the UK's potato industry wouldn't be adequate. No, the truth was that only eight realistic contestants remained.

Here's a list of the eight contenders, some had completed their ten rounds while others had further rounds to complete.

For ease of use I've simply averaged teams' scores to formulate this leaderboard –

64 Irvine/Roulston

64 Dempster/McGilvary

64 Pittendreigh/Adamson*

66 Russon/Douglas*

67 Robb/McFarlane*

68 Duncan/Wood

68 Taylor/McAllan

69 Arthur/Officer

For those marked *, there were only four more opportunities to complete the ten round total. *Pittendreigh/Adamson* had only played eight rounds, but there was sufficient time to qualify comfortably. This therefore left the fourth and final qualifying spot as a likely battle between *myself/Douglas* and *Robb/McFarlane*.

I'm all for an even contest but felt duty-bound to warn Messrs Robb & McFarlane of peculiar happenings at Stonehaven Golf Club in recent years. Superstition has never been a part of my life, I'm quite happy to walk under a ladder and enter a doorway with no.13 above it, I couldn't care a fig. Others are less cavalier however, so I thought I'd point out that, according to folklore, every year during the weekends of late February and early March, gangs of hoodlums wearing balaclavas had been known to accost car owners as they entered the driveway of Stonehaven Golf Club. A peculiar, yet noteworthy, aspect of these confrontations had been that they were only dished out to gentlemen carrying the surnames *'Robb'* and *'MacFarlane'*, and ALWAYS ended with *a severe thrashing of the victims to within an inch of their lives.* I mention this only in passing since, I repeat, I'm not superstitious, but that said, it might have been deemed irresponsible to ignore such a warning were your name to be Robb or MacFarlane. Some might suggest that for them to cock a snook at this warning might have invited trouble. I'll leave it there but all things considered, I knew that if I were them *i wouldn't risk being within a million miles of Stonehaven golf club for the next month or so.* Just sayin' like.

As for the Singles competition, it began with eighty seven entrants. Months of freezing fingers and icicled extremities later, fourteen players remained with a realistic chance of being amongst the twelve qualifiers for the grand final. Most of the front runners appeared safe but a sprinkling of challengers were coming up on the rails so there was still plenty to play for.

The contenders were as follows (their average stableford scores provided).

S McGhie	39
IP Smith	37
S Hutcheon	37*
G Docherty	36
A Darragh	36
C Nicol	36*
M Ritchie	35
D Hepburn	35
AD Smith	35
J Nowak	35
K Gordon	35
G Forrester	34
J Christie	34
P McRobb	34*

*not completed ten rounds yet

Another thirteen players could still complete the requisite ten rounds in time but I'm not wasting space naming them, they were toast. I'd eat my hat if any of them qualified, indeed I'd play the gully in a leopardskin thong using a plastic cricket bat and a medicine ball. In the Winter. No offence, but Rory couldn't drag it back from where these herberts found themselves, they'd be better off staying at home watching Grandstand or cleaning the motor ready for work on Monday.

However, no competition is complete without its also rans. Mention must be made of the hapless couple of dozen who bailed from the tournament having completed no more than two of the minimum ten rounds. The winter league seemed a good idea at the time didn't it gentlemen? That's until you realised it meant rolling out of bed in sub-zero temperatures to thin so many iron shots that you couldn't feel your fingers anymore. The prize to the most random entrant, who will remain nameless, goes to the fellow who waited until week eight to make his debut and promptly called it quits after that one solitary round. As object lessons in futility go, this rivals my attempt, in January, to climb Ben Mohr wearing plimsolls.

CHAPTER TWENTY TWO

'Yes it sure has been a long hard climb'
Bob Dylan

Round 10 – March 5th 2016

Today's round encapsulated what winter league golf is all about. The conditions were deplorable, only a handful of us braved the weather, but we were rewarded with a good laugh and a real sense of achievement. It's a shame for the collection of grinning herberts that lined the clubhouse windows from the comfort of their armchairs as we set off, they don't know what they're missing. A spot of rain shouldn't put Stonehaven members off, are they mice or men? I'll leave someone else to decide after checking their droppings.

Reprehensibly, my winter league partner Keith Douglas was also ready to park himself in the clubhouse rather than play. His face was a picture when I emerged from the car park at 9.30am, pushing my trolley into view, head to toe in waterproofs, ready for action. He greeted me wearing casual clothes and moccasins, assuming we weren't playing.

'F*ck sake Russon, I'm nae playin in this' came his typically cantankerous greeting.

I wasn't impressed. 'It's the winter league Douglas, the clue's in the title. Get changed you wimp, we're playin.'

He shuffled off to the changing rooms, tail between his legs, while I exchanged pleasantries with our impending playing partners. One of them, Martin, was equally as reluctant to play as Keith, "don't do rain, meh, no fun this, glasses get wet, should be in my bed etc etc.' When Douglas returned from the locker room, the chuntering between the two of them reached a crescendo, their resistance however was futile, there was no way I wasn't playing after all the hassle I'd gone through to get clearance for this round of golf. My good lady wife had a prior commitment which I had trumped, my attendance at the golf club earning me several marks in her debit column.

Thankfully, Martin's partner, Colin, was as enthusiastic about a game as I was, so we commenced our round with a modicum of good humour. Colin agreed that golf in adverse weather conditions makes you feel alive, walking into the teeth of a wind, driving rain against your face, feeling at one with nature, you can't beat it. Douglas didn't share our enthusiasm, his face tripping him for the first four holes until he finally got a grip of himself. I suggested he buggered off home and leave me to it after he'd skulked his way through the first three holes, but he explained he wanted to stick around to watch me suffer.

Martin lasted four holes before throwing in the towel. By then Douglas had cheered up a little having witnessed my golf trolley disappear upside down into a bunker, the shallow no-mark couldn't get his camera out quick enough. My trolley has no brakes, if I leave it on a slope the damn thing takes a trip, it made a dash for the cliffs from the 17th fairway a few months ago and later on in today's round departed in pursuit of the railway track by the 10th before capsizing in the rough.

Stoney weather plays cat and mouse with you. After the 8th hole the weather cheered up a little, persuading me to remove my waterproof jacket, but by the time I reached the 9th green my coat was back on, the brief respite from rain short lived. We were in two minds whether to play the field (9th-12th) in proper sequence. Play had slowed up and we wanted to play the gully first (13th-15th), to avoid slow traffic, but Keith's phone call to the clubhouse while we waited on the 7th tee persuaded us not to, the feedback suggesting we might be contravening rules. As it turned out, play speeded up anyway, the twosome in front of us walked in after the 11th and the fourball in front of them followed suit after the 12th due to the diabolical conditions.

In the event, Douglas appeared to enjoy the remainder of the round in a gallows humour kind of way. My trolley mishaps and the madness of playing golf in such atrocious weather seemed to cheer him up, plus we were putting a good score together, which helped. Following my imperious birdie on the 1st, we'd exchanged pars right up until the 11th where he birdied to put us two under. I'd contributed the pars on the tougher holes (5th, 9th and 12th) while he nudged in pars on the simpler ones. He chunked his tee shot embarrassingly on the 7th, only just keeping it in bounds, but somehow scrambled a par, this aside, he largely left me to rescue our card once again.

Colin was soldiering on, tolerating both the conditions and routine abuse that Douglas and I shared. Our day in court approached, but we were duty bound to complete our winter league obligations, so endured each other's company through gritted teeth. We almost had a fight on the 13th tee when he threatened not to play the gully, claiming he was fed up of me taking all the glory for our scores there in recent weeks. I talked him out of this petty lunacy but needn't have bothered, he bogied the 14th after a minor lapse on my part required him to step up to the plate. Perversely however, his failure encouraged my resolve and I atoned for his pathetic three putt on the 14th by notching birdies on 16 and 17 to have us three under as we stood on the last tee.

A number of folk had remained in the warmth of the clubhouse and were looking on as we teed off on the 18th. I lofted an admirable 6-iron onto the green and stood aside for Douglas to try and match me. He didn't. The moment it struck the ball, his club left his hands and disappeared fifty yards down the fairway. The imbecile had managed to throw his club almost as far as he'd hit his ball. He whinged about having wet hands or some such while onlookers guffawed, he then scurried away to retrieve his club, but his second shot wasn't much better, crawling onto the green to leave him a thirty footer. Miraculously however, he drained his putt before I had chance to tap in for my par and we ended with a triumphant 63 which might well cement our place in the winter league final.

The moral of today's story? Get out there and play. It might be wet, it might be cold, but after a week's hard work you owe it to yourself to get some exercise, embrace what nature throws at you and give yourself a few hours fresh air, away from the hurly burly of life. Get up there, get golfing, grow a pair or buy yourself a handbag gentlemen.

CHAPTER TWENTY THREE

'I need the ways and means to get through'
Teenage Fanclub

Serious Bit Alert

March 9th 2016 was the 12th anniversary since I last took a drink. I wanted to share this in case you or a loved one is experiencing problems with alcohol. If I can stop, anyone can stop.

Alcohol entered my life abruptly and took hold until I depended on it like children depend on their mother's milk. It tricked its way in and gave me a new found courage to 'earn' my place amongst peers. Soon it became an anaesthetic, a subconscious self medication when life crowded in on me. Alcohol is a chameleon, appealing to you when you celebrate, commiserate, relax or panic. It's a reward after a hard day, a soother, a familiar friend, a 'go to' response, gradually it burrows it's way in until becoming a way of life, a dependency, your answer to everything. Once you're in its grip, it takes you years to recognise the fact, by which time you're utterly dependent. Denial pervades alcoholics. Only when the alcoholic accepts he or she is powerless over it can steps be taken to address the condition, the tragedy is that most will never acknowledge their addiction. Equally tragic is that only 7% of those attempting sobriety actually sustain it.

What did alcohol do for me? It gave me occasional fun. It also gave me pallid skin, watery eyes, painful kidneys, day long hangovers, trembles, lack of concentration and a damaged liver. It gave me a collection of friends who turned out to be nothing of the sort, they were just drinking partners. It ruined family gatherings; I made an exhibition of myself at my son's christening, missed my Granny's memorial service, was ejected from football matches and rock concerts, missed holidays, ruined holidays, the list goes on and on. I slept on park benches having lost my way home, turned up drunk to meetings, ruined friendships, alienated family, lost all sense of what life was truly about. I missed out on so much that the list would be endless.

Close family and friends suffer even more, constantly picking up the pieces, feeling helpless as they watch a loved one drown in an ocean of booze fuelled regret. We alcoholics are incredibly selfish, nothing comes before us and our drink, not even our children. We're manipulative, saying anything to pacify family, to shut them up, finding ways to facilitate our drinking and excuse our behaviour. We surround ourselves with sympathetic ears who listen to us when we say sorry, we know they'll be there the next time and the time after that. Drink is the goal and nothing will get in the way. This leaves family despairing, bewildered, at their wits end. If you're close to a loved one struggling with alcohol dependency then please access the following website, there's support available to you www.al-anonuk.org.uk

So how have I managed twelve years of sobriety? Well all the glory goes to God and the grace he has shown me. When all seemed lost, I reluctantly followed up on an acquaintance's urge for me to 'try church' and eventually this brought into my life a man called Peter, who became a counsellor, a friend, and the man who taught me to live by the mantra; 'People and Places', – if you mix with the same people and frequent the same places, nothing will change, if you put recovery at the centre of your life, make root and branch alterations to the way you live, there's a chance. Peter encouraged me to share the faith in God that he had and it's this alone that has pulled me through, this I know because when I tried sobriety under my own steam, it was a dead loss.

The riches available to those who get sober are incalculable. The simple things in life, once taken for granted or ignored, become new discoveries, mini miracles. Colours become vibrant, the air smells fresh, flavours are tasted, family and friends are pleased to see you, energy replaces fatigue and you stand taller. It's a rebirth, a new life and it's priceless.

I kicked the backside out of it for nineteen years, boozing my way to the brink of oblivion before mercifully finding a way out. Believe me when I say that if I can do it, anyone can do it. There are agencies who can help provided you want it enough, drop me a line and I'll happily put you in touch. naffgolfer@ gmail.com

---

CHAPTER TWENTY FOUR

'I'm tellin ya bro someday it's all gonna hit ya'
The Charlatans

There were twenty one pubs in Stoney when I lived in the town and I visited the bulk of them before leaving in 1986. Given I was barely seventeen by then that's quite an achievement/ indictment. My first drink was in the Ship Inn since all of the other establishments would turn me away, rightly, for being under age. Many's the time I suffered the leg pulling of friends as I took my seat, 'Nae drinkin' Russon?!', my glass of coke sat forlornly alongside their lagers.

Miraculously though, the Ship Inn served me. A pool table was situated next to a window overlooking the harbour, so we'd pull the curtains at the earliest available opportunity so not to be spotted by our parents. I worked part-time as a glass collector in the Marine pub a couple of doors down from The Ship, thanks to my father's introduction to the landlord, Phil Duncan. The Marine was the busier of the two pubs, it served real ale and good food while the Ship was purely a drinker's pub.

I soon got hooked on drinking and gradually moved on from the exclusivity of the Ship Inn when we found ourselves accepted in The Eldergrove, The Royal (occasionally) and The Star (or 'Starry'), provided we let Fergy get the drinks in while we cowered in the corner. This isn't to glorify under-age drinking by the way, the eventual consequence of this introduction to alcohol you're now fully appraised of. Typically I'd have a couple of pints of Tennent's lager then move onto the lesser of two evils, southern comfort and lemonade or vodka and orange.

I liked neither but given I couldn't cope with the volume of lager and hadn't the courage to order coke in view of my peers, there was no choice but to nurse weakened spirits. After a while I discovered McEwans Export, or 'Heavy', which I enjoyed more than was good for me, sufficiently to drop the shorts (so to speak) and continue drinking even when my bursting gut said enough was enough. 'Heavy' became my drink of choice, whether on draught in pubs or in cans at parties.

Even after eighteen months of weekend drinking, it was something of a surprise when not asked to prove my age by publicans, I've always looked younger than I am so at sixteen years of age had no right whatever to expect anything stronger than lemonade and a packet of scampi fries. There were plenty of tumbleweed moments along the way but I got to know which bar staff would serve me and which wouldn't, for instance the bloke who looked like Butler off *On the Buses* would never serve me in The Ship so I'd sit in the lounge and wait for my drink to be bought through by a friend, however the old wifie in the Belvedere barely looked above her glasses when serving, I could have been an infant baboon and been served a pint. I let my mates do the buying most of the time though, since they all looked older and were shaving, I think I was nineteen before I took a razor out and that was only to deal with a hairy mole on my shoulder.

There were seven of us who'd go out drinking; me, Jason Waddleton, Chas Wilkinson, Chas Francis, Andrew Dickens, Fergy and Paul Crandon. There were other more occasional socialites including Jamie Collie, Phil Fowles and Jamie McCaskill, and a group of older ones who intimidated the hell out of me, probably because I was pre-pubescent and English while they were mannies and Scottish, their names I won't provide because even now they haunt me. It was tough mixing or semi-mixing in certain circles, I was always the hanger-on truth be told, on the periphery of the group rather than at the epicentre, so acted up in an attempt to ingratiate myself. Football hooliganism was rife around that time and English hooligans were looked upon with a warped sense of awe so my reports from Villa matches I'd occasionally travel to, were embellished ludicrously to my waiting audience, it got me noticed. But boasting about thugs from Birmingham wasn't enough to have me entirely welcomed into the fold so I found another route; excessive drinking. If there was a Friday night out or a party, Russon could be relied upon to get minket and provide the entertainment. It wasn't big and certainly wasn't clever but when you're a young adolescent in the company of confident, big lads, you search for a way to be accepted and drink gave me an identity, albeit a misguided one. I had no confidence in myself, had very low self esteem so seized upon what I saw as an opportunity to be part of the gang. Pathetic really. Girls weren't impressed. The ones our group mixed with, or attempted to mix with, were pretty mature for their age and their perception of me hardly improved when I'd pitch up at their soirees barely able to make it over the threshold. Vicky, Kate, Shelley, Emma, all of them looked upon me with pity, although I know that only in retrospect, at the time I thought I was cool. Occasionally they'd plan a party when their parents were away and invite us over, they stayed in pleasant houses and apartments, beautiful décor and spotless surfaces. They'd have a drink in town, not necessarily an alcoholic one, then return to prepare for guests, most of whom had the decency to pitch up at a reasonable hour and behave themselves. I on the other hand remained in the Ship until late then shuffled to the party where I'd either crash out, vomit or offend. I was, to put it mildly, a complete arse, and I'm ashamed to say that's largely how I remained for the next eighteen years. I'd served my apprenticeship, I'd later discover, in a career of functioning alcoholism.

Of course all roads in those days lead to the Commodore Hotel on a Friday night, a legendary gathering for the young folk. The Commy was a hotel by Mineralwell Park however it met its demise in 2002, levelled to make way for flats. Commy nights were the highlight of the week, an opportunity to have a drink, mess about with your mates and if you were lucky, get a feel off a girl behind the long draped curtains. In truth only two of these eventualities would come to pass and neither were the latter. I'd accomplish the first two objectives pretty comfortably but stage three was quite out of the question, unless some quine was desperate and didn't mind a drunken English bloke falling asleep upon her shoulder.

A typical Friday would develop thus; I'd shuffle home from school, usually walking down the Slug Road with Shelley Lockheart or Jim Acton, or alone, then down Evan Street to Barclays Street where I'd nip into Double D's amusement arcade for a game of Defender or a quid on the fruit machines. Cash duly frittered, I'd walk on home to Salmon Lane and raid the cupboards ahead of my parents return from work. I'd be alone because my brother, Stu, was the world's slowest returnee from school, where he'd go I didn't know, sometimes to Ally & Colin Still's house. Our other brother Chris would be at a child minders or with Margaret Soutar and her son Alexs who lived on the High Street. I'd be scoffing digestive biscuits, mini pizzas and cheese on toast, preparing for the night's festivities, Jason would telephone to confirm arrangements, probably 7pm outside the cannon statue on the high street. I'd shower and change into standard soccer casual uniform (not that I was a soccer casual but I dressed like one when not in my golf gear); stone washed jeans with the frayed hem dragging on the ground, blue 'Kickers' shoes (red optional), plain Lacoste polo shirt (any colour) and a side parting with hair close cropped at the sides and back. I owned some of this uniform but not all, my attempts to compensate for the shortfall often attracting derision. For example I had Kicker moccasins, not the pucker shoes, and my hair was completely atrocious. I sit here at the ripe old age of forty six and can say without risk of contradiction that I have never possessed a hairstyle. My hair is thin, grows quickly and becomes a bowlheid if I'm not careful, since the age of twelve I've attacked it with all manner of product in an attempt to develop an acceptable structure, always I fail. Nothing prevents it from dropping like a stone into straight lines from the crown of my head so I look like I'm wearing a set of undrawn curtains. Gel, mousse, clay, you name it I've tried it until my lowest ebb was reached when turning to my mother's hairspray. One evening I delivered half a can of the stuff to my faltering flick until it became so firm you could crack an egg on it. I later ate with Jasons family at the Marine, drank my fill, yodelled out of the taxi window on the way home and woke up the next morning with my hair looking like the nutty professor off that Michael J Fox film. My barnet standing vertically, sprinkled with diced carrots.

But back to Commy nights. Half a dozen of us would alight on the High Street and saunter down to The Ship, Chas and I scurrying through to the lounge because we looked the youngest, Dick and Fergy ordering the drinks. The lounge was usually empty, perhaps the odd middle aged couple having a quiet drink, and we'd settle in for a couple of hours before walking into town to nominate a pub we might stand a chance of getting served in. The Star would be touch and go and The Royal too, if we didn't fancy our chances we'd buy some cans and drink them at Mineralwell. Most of my mates would be tipsy but not drunk, I on the other hand would be weaving so couldn't guarantee admission, alcohol wasn't served in the Commy so you had to load up prior to entry. Once inside I can't remember much to be honest except the over-riding sensation of feeling utterly alone despite the crowds of people. I was drunk, immature and a liability, friends and strangers body swerving me and understandably so. This was a sign of things to come in adulthood, drink becoming my tragedy.

Here's a list of Stonehaven pubs that I either frequented or attempted to –

The Ship Inn

The White Heather – Fishermans pub, no chance of getting served here, the regulars would have me for breakfast.

The Marine – given I worked there as a glass collector, because I wasn't old enough to serve alcohol, I had absolutely no hope of getting a drink (unless with a meal in the restaurant, a perverse law saying you could drink alcohol if dining and over sixteen).

The Mill Inn – I had many a happy night here. Tucked away behind a petrol station, it wasn't easy to find and as a consequence, struggled for business. Several blokes in their late teens/early twenties drank there, and since we knew a few of them, we felt sufficiently emboldened to drink there too. That was until a televised Scotland v England football match when myself and Phil Fowles were naïve enough to celebrate England's victory, it was some time before we showed our faces in there again. The Mill Inn also boasted the coolest named football team in the district, AC Mill Inn.

The Crown – I had a drink in there once or twice but it was difficult because I lived virtually opposite it. At lunchtime the bar staff would be seeing me returning home in my school uniform and in the evening I'd bowl in there asking for a pint of Heavy, it'd didn't really work. It was also rather too close to home, my brother Stu would only need look out of his bedroom window and there I'd be, mind you I doubt he'd have said anything. My Dad wouldn't have been able to see that far, his eyesight being dreadful, but my Mum could and that's a risk I wasn't going to take.

The Royal Hotel – this was run by the parents of a lad in my year at school (I'm thinking Jamie McPherson?) and while he wasn't part of our little crew, I didn't want to put him in the awkward position of not grassing me up. His parents sold the place however, which encouraged occasional visits, usually upstairs to the function room. I have a very vivid memory of a conversation in here with Emma Laird. If I had my time again and made a different decision following our chat, my life would surely have turned out differently. It was an identical conversation to one I had with another friend, Dan Slater, seventeen years later. There I stood with a glass of vodka and orange, looking like a child, feeling as lonely as ever, desperately trying to impress my peers by drinking alcohol and trying to be clever. Emma knew that drinking wasn't really me, that I was acting up, showing off, striving to be someone I didn't honestly want to be in the first place. I remember feeling trapped in my own existence, I'd painted myself into a corner and didn't have sufficient belief or wherewithal to extricate myself, it'd take a virtual rebirth and I wasn't strong enough to attempt it. Emma implored me to stop the rot, to start making tough decisions, alcohol abuse wasn't big and wasn't clever. I wish I'd have listened.

The Grapevine – a wine bar opposite La Cucina, rather a hip place to be. It's design was before it's time really, standing apart from all the other bars in town with its low lighting, dark wooden flooring, open plan tables and chairs rather than booths or bar stools, attractive furnishings, modern artwork. I've no idea how long it lasted but it hadn't been open long before I moved back to Birmingham in 1986. I'm ashamed to confess that Jason and I proved that under eighteens aren't mature enough to drink by daubing various slogans on the walls leading to the lavatories. How we didn't get tumbled I'll never know, there can't have been many people in Stoney scrawling AVFC and NUFC on bistro bar walls.

The Star – or more accurately, the 'Starry'. During my five years living in Stonehaven I became aware of several words that Brummies shouldn't attempt if they wanted to avoid the sniggering of locals. 'Starry' was one of these words, as was 'murder', 'birdie' and 'clipe.' It took me a while to get with the programme. The Star was a touch and go pub for teenagers, if you knew your place, had one quick drink very early in the evening and then buggered off without fuss, you were tolerated. Get cocky though and it was good night.

The Hook & Eye – see **The White Heather.**

The Market Bar – there was absolutely zero chance of spotty teenagers getting a drink in here, it was renowned as a proper boozers bar, set apart for seasoned drinkers who'd swill their way through their every waking hour. We'd have got laughed out of the place if we set foot in there. Definitely one to miss.

My Place – I can't recall ever going in here and, again, I feel this may have been a sensible move. Some bars you'll try your luck in, this one I didn't, it gave me the willies and I sensed that had I entered I'd be delivered back onto the street five minutes later after a good hiding.

St Leonards Hotel – one of several hotels in the town with a lounge bar, we enjoyed occasional success here and there'd often be a function for us to gatecrash. Tickets were sold for drinks and stovies at Hogmanay before folk moved on to the fireballs.

The Heugh Hotel – I never went there, it always looked too austere for us to have a chance of getting served and was situated out of the way, up on the Slugger, a long walk from town. It was a fantastic looking building, but ancient looking, I got the impression that the average resident was 75 years old and we'd get served cocoa from a trolley rather than a beer.

The Station – I drank in there once, got threatened by a burly guy from Brickfield and didn't go back, except to graffiti the nearby train station walls with Jason, for which we were rightly punished.

The County – Another hotel but bigger than many of the others, had its own squash courts and gym. I occasionally played squash then had a drink, but it's tricky paying reduced junior fees for your squash then ordering a pint of Heavy. This hotel was levelled for flats too.

The Eldergrove – ah, now you're talking. This was a very popular spot for friends and I to meet and on the odd occasion, take a quine for the evening. A bright, airy room with a tiny little bar in the corner, the type of snug bar you'd see in someone's house if they were ostentatious. It was a wonderful retreat, we never misbehaved in there or abused their hospitality, we didn't want to offend them.

The Belvedere – Tucked away by the library on Evan Street, another hotel with a small bar. It was very dated, the décor and seating from yesteryear, tartan tapestries, grouse statues and bagpipes hanging from the walls. The bar was rarely busy apart from residents enjoying a quiet drink. I've got a photo somewhere of me drinking in there while wearing a Villa shirt tightly stretched over my beer belly. I was only seventeen and thought I looked good, what a clown.

If I had my time again, I'd walk past every one of these pubs and do something else instead of pretending to be an adult. Don't do it kids, there's a better life than weaning yourself on booze and Stonehaven offers plenty of worthy alternatives to the youth of today.

CHAPTER TWENTY FIVE

'And when you want to live, how do you start,
where do you go, who do you need to know?'
The Smiths

Serious bit #2

During the 1982-86 period, Fetteresso Church was a building I walked past on the way to school. These days it's rather more than that.

I became a Christian in 2002 after thirty three years of agnosticism bordering on atheism. No, get it straight, it was atheism. I didn't believe in God but then again, can't remember a genuine confrontation with the issue. I didn't believe in anything really, I just drifted along on choppy waters, good days intertwined with bad, life wasn't great, but bearable. My existence mirrored my father's approach to golf, a damage limitation exercise, provided I wasn't double bogeying I'd be happy with that. No high expectations, no ambition above my station, just a grim march to the finish and, if I was lucky, there'd be a bonus par or birdie along the way.

There then came a period, towards the end of my nineteen year drinking binge, when the good days were crowded out entirely by bad. To continue the golfing analogy, I was double bogeying every hole and throwing in the odd triple. My existence had become a series of regrets, embarrassments, apologies and disasters. Life was completely unmanageable as I battled helplessly with alcohol addiction. I'd left my wife, been separated from my children, experienced a spell in a psychiatric hospital having been deemed a danger to myself, in short I'd become an utter shambles.

A few weeks after my release from hospital, I returned to work and held a business meeting with a chap in Stoke-on-Trent, his name Philip Hall, owner of a timber company that bought products from the sawmill that employed me. We met for coffee at the Holiday Inn off the M6.

I looked dreadful. Palid eyes, blotchy skin, bloated face, shaking with the DT's, sweating despite it being winter, in possession of a thunderous hangover. We greeted one another, exchanged pleasantries and were barely seated when Philip fired a question at me out of leftfield.

'What's going on in your life Alex? You look awful.'

I was somewhat taken aback, laughing it off with a 'how kind of you to notice' type of answer. But he meant it, he wouldn't be brushed off and continued his line of enquiry. I'd never had a relative stranger take a genuine interest in me like this and was thrown, why would he want to share my worries and woes? What was his agenda?

'You look like you've the weight of the world on your shoulders, what's happening?'

Caught off guard, with no time to concoct a sanitised reply or dream up a false narrative, I let it all tumble out, giving him my backstory warts and all. There were plenty of warts. I explained the pain my marriage breakup had caused, the hollowness of life when your children are removed from your daily routine, the terror of a legal journey through family courts to re-establish contact, I'd not seen them in four months now. Alcohol was my anaesthetic, my dependency upon it had intensified, each day commencing with a hangover, I worked from home so had every opportunity to drink myself through the morning with a telephone in one hand and a can of Stella in the other, before I took residence in The Duke Of York pub for the afternoon. My life was utterly chaotic, completely out of control.

Phil didn't interrupt, he sat patiently. So many people listen but don't listen, just waiting for a pause to exploit, diving in to interrupt when you take a breath. Philip though was listening, truly listening, and when I finished, he fixed his eyes on mine and said 'And have you asked God to help you?"

I thought he was joking, perhaps trying to lighten the atmosphere given I'd become tearful while delivering my war story, until he asked again, 'have you asked God to help you?"

Flippin 'eck he was serious. Had I asked God to help me? Had I hell. What God? I didn't believe there was one, and if there was, which was a stretch of the imagination too far for any sane human being, how on earth would he allow me to get myself into this state? What kind of God looks on impassively while people struggle so badly? Wars, floods, famines, poverty, the list was endless and yet I was to believe there was a God? Here I was at rock bottom, emptying my soul to a virtual stranger who was now exploiting my vulnerability, jabbering on about God, goblins and fairies. I told him I didn't appreciate his question and could we talk about something else, but he wasn't finished.

'You've chosen to live life your way Alex and it's not taken you to a happy place has it? Carry on in this direction and I'm fearful for you, who knows where it might end?' Philip spoke with compassion, without judgement, he wasn't pitying me, he had genuine empathy which took me aback, it's unusual listening to a stranger explain he cares for you. But I wasn't having this God stuff.

'Some God who lets me get into this shape Philip. I don't believe in God, how could I? I'm a wreck.'

'Speaking to him would be a start' replied Philip, 'tell him how you feel. He isn't a bearded old man sailing along on the clouds, he's a living God, he wants to be involved in the grot and the good going on in your life. He's your father in heaven, he loves you, yearns for a relationship with you, but it's a two way street. When you were a kid, how could your Dad help you unless you communicated with him? If you fell off your bike, he couldn't patch you up unless you went to him. Plasters, juice and sympathy don't fall from the sky, your Dad would dust you down and show you how to ride so you wouldn't fall another time, but if you did, he'd be there to pick up the pieces again. So it is with your father in heaven. He's there for you, but relationships are the responsibility of two parties, he can't help you if you block him out.'

Cute words, pleasant concept, but I remained cynical. I'd been to church sporadically as a kid, but the whole God thing hadn't touched me one iota. I'd tolerated Sunday school when my parents were attending church because they wanted my youngest brother christened (the vicar had asked them to at least show willing before formally committing their child to God). Beyond this I'd been to weddings in draughty churches and was quite happy to leave it there.

'You Christians, always get us when we're down don't you?' I was maddened that he'd had the audacity to introduce religion, unsolicited.

'Yip' he replied, smiling. 'God's there for you any time at all but particularly when you need him most. Forget about churches, old fashioned stone buildings and men in robes with dog collars around their necks. Think about God, a being, someone you can have a living relationship with. You've had a pretty tough time living life your way, why not entertain the possibility that there is more to life than this, you really have nothing to lose.'

We spoke some more before parting, Philip shaking my hand and looking warmly into my eyes with an expression that I won't forget, one of compassion, peacefulness and certainty. I felt reassured, becalmed, but most of all I felt hopeful. He'd meant every word he'd said, a quietly spoken, mild mannered, middle aged gent with no agenda other than to encourage his fellow man, it was inspiring. I walked back to the car in a daze, sat, cried, slept, cried some more and decided to give this thing a try.

I went to a local church the following Sunday, I was that desperate. I sat through the service in an attitude of cynicism and low expectation, taking nothing from the experience whatsoever before heading for the exit, ready to write the whole farrago off as a bad job. I was heading home, the fridge contained cans of Stella with my name on them. As I reached the main door of the church though, I was intercepted by the vicar, John Reeves, who'd made a beeline from the front. He asked me who I was and where I lived, with the same warmth and compassion that Philip had when listening to me earlier in the week. Nice of him I thought, pleasant chap, but I'm off home for a beer.

A couple of days later there was a knock at the door, I answered to find John Reeves standing there, wondering if I fancied a coffee. Cutting a long story short, there began a long friendship, John was a great support to me, not least because he illustrated a peace in his life that I desperately wanted for myself, despite his own personal backstory which would strip paint from walls. I gave church another try, enrolled on a course to find out more about this Christian faith caper and joined the church football team. Life began to change, I was still drinking, but it was interrupted by occasional interactions with people who didn't judge me or want anything from me, I felt no pressure amongst them, their lives presented problems for sure, but they appeared to cope so much better, whereas I'd turn to drink.

Gradually life became brighter. The crises continued, but my approach changed. A light came on and flickered, the room remained dark, but light was there nonetheless. There was a new dynamic; hope. A magic wand hadn't been waved nor a healing potion supped, my son and daughter remained withheld from me, alcohol dependency persisted, as did financial strife, but I didn't feel abandoned anymore. I felt a peace, a calmness, my spirit was lifted. People at church wanted to know me, to support me, and it was unconditional, they had no interest other than for my wellbeing. That's where I met Peter who became my alcohol counsellor and my friend. You might refer to these people as Jesus freaks, I know I did, but this Jesus Christ chap of whom they spoke, grabbed me by the short and curlies, straightened me out and hasn't been off my case since, thank God. Life's not been a bed of roses but the thorns don't cause as much pain anymore.

CHAPTER TWENTY SIX

'We all feel a little danger when there's something
in the air'
The Charlatans

Back to the golf. Just one weekend remained for Stonehaven's golfers to qualify for the three winter league finals; *the singles, the doubles gross and doubles nett*. The list of contenders had dwindled to a handful, dozens of early hopefuls long since having their chips. The journey was littered with casualties, their dreams in tatters, their excuses at the ready, their families ashamed.

In a humble and commendable act of inclusivity by the club's tournament leaders, the also rans were invited to form a guard of honour for the leaders, beginning outside the locker room and stretching all the way to the first tee. It was the least the hundred or so bridesmaids could do having stunk the course out all winter and, if they hung around long enough, they might learn a thing or two. In the event, the tribute didn't materialise, their loss.

The Singles

Seven players remained in contention, the best four average scores to qualify.

S McGhie	38.9 points
IP Smith	36.8
S Hutcheon*	36.8
G Docherty	36.7
M Ritchie	35.9
J Nowak	35.7
A Darragh	35.5

*S Hutcheon was sitting pretty but had no grounds for complacency. He was the only one yet to complete ten rounds so if he took a dose of the squits after a bad Friday night curry, his incapacitation would give opponents an opportunity to sail past him.

The Doubles (gross)

Two other gentlemen touching cloth were Pittendreigh & Adamson. They too had one more round still to register and while in third place just now, could yet crash and burn. The top two looked nailed on for qualification but leaders Dempster/ McGillvary faced a steward's enquiry after registering a highly improbable 58 in the previous week's horrendous conditions. If they could break 60 with frozen fingers and grips wetter than an otter's crotch then my name was Donald Duck.

Dempster/McGillvary	61.9 strokes
Irvine/Roulston	63.3
Pittendreigh/Adamson*	64.5
Russon/Douglas	65.0
Arthur/Officer	65.6
McAllan/Taylor	65.7

The Doubles (nett)

McArthur/Henderson	57.0 strokes
Halliday/Campbell	58.7
Duncan/Wood	59.1
Barnett/Simpson	59.8
Starrs/Taylor	60.3
Pittendreigh/Adamson*	60.4

The heat was sure on for Pittendreigh/Adamson. If they made a dog's breakfast of their final round they could dip out on both the scratch and nett competitions, a disappointing end to a winter that promised so much. They were surely bricking it, a pre-match session on the throne beckoned this forthcoming Saturday morning, perhaps for a few others too. The changing room lavatory brush would take some and no mistake.

CHAPTER TWENTY SEVEN

'Well I don't know how it ends up here'
The Thrills

Final Qualifying Round – March 13th 2016

So it all came down to this, the final qualifying round of the 2016 Winter League Doubles. Douglas and I had completed ten rounds but had an opportunity to knock one of the weaker scores off the list with this, our eleventh. We reckoned we needed a three under par total of 63 to virtually guarantee our place in the final although, until all the scores were in at the end of the weekend, we simply wouldn't know.

We got off to a poor start, parring the eminently birdieable first hole despite almost driving the green, and after nine holes we remained only level par. We birdied 10, parred 11 but then the 12th hole looked like derailing us as we locked horns once again. Douglas had offered precious little over the first eight holes and he knew it, his pride was taking a pounding. I was too polite to bring his shortcomings to his attention yet it remained something of an elephant in the room. I'd been sinking putts left, right and centre while he was hacking along and when I finally asked him to pull the finger from his arsehole he didn't take too kindly to the request. We stood on the 12th tee, Douglas's face tripping him, and his mood worsened further when he drove hopelessly into a fairway bunker. Uncharacteristically, I followed by hoicking my drive out of bounds, that's when the trouble started.

'F*ck sake, how did you nae just stick 'een up the middle with your three wood?' grumbled the very herbert who'd just slogged one into a bunker.

'Just put one up the middle? What am I Rory McIlroy now, plonking drives up the middle on demand. I'm not a pro you cretin, I play off 10.'

'But you kent I was in the bunker, you dick' whimpered Douglas.

'That's immaterial. I don't develop a radar for the middle of the fairway each time you find sand.'

He shuffled off muttering to himself and proceeded to scrape a bogey before stomping to the next tee, slagging me off all the way.

'The 12th is stroke index one Douglas, the hardest hole on the course. Do you honestly expect me to magic a par four out of nothing?'

''at's nae the point, you just needed to keep it in play, you're f*cking brainless Russon.'

This futile exchange continued until the 13th tee at which point he threatened to walk off the course. Our playing partners talked him out of such petulance and mercifully, he birdied the very next hole which pepped up his mood. A further birdie at 17 brought us home with a respectable 64, a shot short of our target but hopefully enough to qualify.

The following day, after a rapid exchange of confessional text messages between the competing pairs, much of it deliberately inaccurate, it was discovered that we had indeed won through to the final and done so by two shots. At first I didn't know whether to believe it, I've had my leg pulled so many times it looks like I wear stilts, but confirmation reached me late on Sunday evening, signalling a celebratory hot chocolate and accompanying Garibaldi. I know how to rock n roll.

Naturally, when one succeeds by a mere two shots after three months of golf, one's mind is drawn to those pivotal moments where qualification may have been won and lost. The good scores in adverse conditions, the bravely holed three footers, the fairway splitting drives when your partner's dumped his on the railway line. To this end, one specific memory stands out.

Twas the 18th hole of our seventh round and once again I'd been the warrior of our partnership while Douglas had been the weasel. He'd been provoking me over the impending court action, his lawyer had buoyed him up during the week by assuring him of an open and shut case, even to the point of suggesting I faced a custodial sentence. Said lawyer had also implored him to complete our winter league obligations since this would stand his legal case in better stead, so our partnership staggered on despite the obvious animosity. On this particular day Douglas had played so pathetically that I suspected sabotage, he appeared to be doing his utmost to ensure we wouldn't qualify for the final. This was never better illustrated when on the 18th hole he sent his tee shot miles out of bounds after selecting a five-iron where an eight-iron was needed. Turning to me with a stupid grin on his face he goaded 'over to you Russon.' His lamentable attitude didn't intimate me however, it merely encouraged me, and I nervelessly secured the four that, in the event, gained us a passage into the final (yes I know the last is a par three but had I notched a six instead we'd have been out of the competition, let's not be churlish).

145

So there we have it. Despite legal action and a near fist fight on the 13th tee, the Russon/Douglas partnership lives to fight one final day, final being the operative word. We stand toe to toe with three other doubles teams next Saturday to play for the Winter League Championship 2016. Two aspects of this event have me partying in my pants; 1) I'm playing in my first final since the Sutton Coldfield Cub Scouts 5-a-side football competition at Wyndley Leisure Centre in 1977 and 2) It's the last time I'll have to play golf with Keith Douglas ever again. It won't be the last time I see him though, the date has been set for our court case.

CHAPTER TWENTY EIGHT

'All you cynics and you mimics, all you losers and abusers, wasting all my precious energy'
Ian Brown

The day before the grand final, a local newspaper published my preview…

Described by many as golf's fifth major, the Stonehaven winter league reaches its climax this weekend. Ryder Cup points are up for grabs, but the pride in lifting this prestigious trophy is reason enough for the finalists to strain every sinue over Stoney's hallowed turf. Somewhat controversially, the event has been billed merely as world golf's season curtain raiser one month ahead of the Masters, something of an impertinence. The SGC winter league is nobody's bitch, Amen corner doesn't hold a candle to Stoney's gully and as closing holes go, Augusta doesn't have a centuries old graveyard next to it, we do. It'll come in handy tomorrow, we're going to bury McGilvary and Dempster in there after they complete the biggest choke since Greg Norman in 1996.

Yes Douglas and I are in the final and we won't be taking any prisoners. Well I won't anyway, if rumours about Douglas's pre-match plans are to be believed, I doubt he'll be capable of lifting a club come the morning. I'm proposing a light pasta salad for my supper followed by an early night with a cool flannel placed upon my forehead, Douglas, however, has his name on a crate of Becks and a 4am taxi return from an Aberdeen casino. With such wanton disregard for golf's first set piece event of the year, is it any wonder he's facing defeat in his libel case against me? My criticisms of him on the blog 'Stoney Baloney' are irrefutable and he'll discover as such in the sheriff's court. But I digress.

There are three categories to be contested tomorrow and each is there for the taking. Qualifying scores are carried into the final so some competitors hold a slight advantage, however one cannot discount the power of nerves, all it takes is a panic filled grubber off the first tee to shatter your confidence for the rest of the round. Take Messrs McGilvary and Dempster for example, word has it they've already booked Aberdeen's swankiest restaurant so they can celebrate in style with their families tomorrow night. Jumping the gun a little aren't we gentlemen? Let's hope humble pie is on the menu after you're pipped to the trophy by a barrage of Russon birdies, I'll buy you both a knife and fork to mark the occasion. Don't throw your victory speech away though, I'll be needing that to light my cigar.

Final day nerves will pervade the singles competition too. The leader, S McGhie, lies two stableford points ahead of the field after a dominant display in qualifying, but a dose of the eebie jeebies on the first couple of holes and that lead can evaporate in a flash. Who's to say he won't shank one onto the 18th green off the 1st tee and dump one down the cliffs on the 2nd? Before you know it his lead's gone and his opponents can smell blood and diarrhea in equal measure. It's a ruthless business top level golf, no place for pansies, and Finals day sees the cream rise to the top. The doubles nett competition finds McArthur & Henderson peering from atop the leaderboard with an advantage of two shots, but again, this is the slimmest of comfort blankets, more of a comfort napkin.

The doubles competitions are intriguing in terms of the varying dynamics evident between the respective playing partners. Some partnerships are warm and friendly, plenty of back slapping and encouraging words, other partnerships, Douglas and I for example, smoke with hateful animosity yet somehow work. Douglas hates my guts, similarly I wouldn't urinate on him if he were on fire, however our low regard for one another matters little, it's the digits written on the scorecard that count, regardless of the fact that nine times out of ten those digits are mine. We may wish a pox upon each other's houses, but there we sit in the penultimate playing group on Finals day, Sky's cameras watching our every move. The three teams ahead of us may be planning to walk off hand in hand into the sunset, their friendships blossoming as they skip gaily around the course, but has their love-in yet been put to the test? It's easy to be pals when you're nonchalantly nudging your balls around the course during qualification rounds, let's see how supportive they are of each other in the white hot atmosphere of Finals day? The wheat is sorted from the chaff when you reach the business end of golf's fifth major, just watch as these partnerships splinter like trees attacked by an axe. I look forward with relish to the disintegration of our three opponent's partnerships as Douglas and I march grimly on to victory. Golf is about blood and snotters winning, not airy fairy losing. A three shot deficit doesn't intimidate us, we'll have that wiped out before you're lining up your putts on the 4th green Mr McGilvary. By the time you approach the field you'll be in tatters Mr Dempster. You deal in pars, we deal in birdies so stick that up your arris. The fat lady hasn't even waddled onto stage yet gentlemen.

CHAPTER TWENTY NINE

'Don't ever stand aside, don't ever be denied'
Oasis

The Grand Final

In appropriately cold conditions on a gusty Saturday morning, the winter league drew to a close. I'd hoped to spend several pages describing our victorious round however the events don't merit such a tribute. Instead, I'll deliver the bald facts and give you a summary of the details. The winners were -

Singles – M Ritchie
Doubles Nett – N MacArthur / D Henderson
Doubles Gross – B McGilvary / S Dempster *(steward's enquiry)

M Ritchie produced a scintillating final round (44 pts) to pip S McGhie to the post in the Singles and despite a spirited performance by Barnett/Simpson in the *Doubles Nett,* they were trumped by a spectacular final round from MacArthur/Henderson (a nett 52 if you please!)

As regards the doubles gross competition, it's my solemn duty to report that McGilvary/Dempster were reported to the committee with a recommendation that they be stripped of their title. An upstanding citizen of Stonehaven Golf Club (ie. me) felt it only right that an official complaint be lodged regards their conduct and an emergency committee meeting has been convened following my written complaint...

Dear Sirs,

Today, Keith Douglas and I competed in the final of the winter league doubles competition and found ourselves finishing in second place behind Messrs McGilvary & Dempster. I would however like to bring a number of facts to your attention regards the behaviour of this year's 'winners' and implore you to do the only rightful thing, award the trophy to the runners-up instead, (ie. myself and Keith Douglas.)

The conduct of McGilvary & Dempster has been beneath contempt since the beginning of the competition. I don't like to tell tales but someone needs to make you aware of their reprehensible behaviour and I consider it your duty not only to disqualify them from the tournament, but to drum them out of the club altogether. We cannot allow the reputation of Stonehaven Golf Club to be sullied by these individuals, action must be taken.

I present to you the following reasons for their disqualification and look forward to meeting you at the prize giving later in the year. While I think about it, for the purposes of trophy engraving, I take this opportunity to clarify the spelling of my surname, it's 'R U S S O N'.

1. *McGilvary & Dempster were scheduled to commence their final round immediately behind ourselves but instead snuck onto the first tee before us, thereby playing out of turn.*

2. *On the penultimate qualifying weekend, the pair played on a dry, sunny Sunday while the rest of us played on a wet, freezing Saturday. It's not fair.*

3.   *McGilvary quite clearly had his shirt tail hanging out as he began his final round, bringing the reputation of Stonehaven Golf Club into disrepute.*

4.   *The winning scorecard should not be accepted. It was dog eared in one corner and the 'I' in McGilvary's surname was not dotted.*

5.   *Both players failed to pass a drugs test. Granted there wasn't a drugs test to pass but the fact remains, they didn't pass a drugs test.*

6.   *Dempster wheeled his trolley over the corner of the 7th green in round two of qualifying last November, bang out of order. It may not have been him but I'm pretty sure it was.*

7.   *McGilvary exceeded the speed limit when driving into the club car park on the morning of the final.*

8.   *Dempster didn't flush the toilet in the Gents following his pre-match turd.*

For these reasons I believe the McGilvary/Dempster partnership should be relieved of the title and the honour should instead be awarded to myself and Keith Douglas. If you'd rather Douglas didn't share the accolade with me I would accept this as a reasonable compromise.

I await your response.

Yours sincerely

Alex Russon

CHAPTER THIRTY

'See I've already waited too long,
now all my hope is gone'
The Smiths

After several months of bitter wrangling, the libel case between Keith Douglas and myself drew to a close in the Spring of 2016. It was sad for a friendship to end so acrimoniously, our dirty linen being aired in public, but I was compelled to defend myself against his wholly inaccurate claims that I'd lied when describing events on my Winter League blog. We'd known each other for decades and many of our mutual friends had implored us not to go to court, suggesting we strip to the waist for a fistfight on Stonehaven beach instead, anything except litigation. I gave this some serious consideration, however I hadn't the heart to humiliate the man by giving him a good hiding in front of his family and friends, instead I chose to defend myself in an honourable fashion, in a court of law, where the facts could speak for themselves and the legal process could formally vindicate me. I'd rightly claimed Douglas to be the rudest player I'd ever accompanied and a man who'd contributed bugger-all to our winter league runners up position (the committee had thrown out my appeal against McGilvary & Dempster). These were stone cold facts, as was the malfunction of his personal hygiene. I had irrefutable photographic evidence proving his inability to reach the humps on the first hole and the testimony of several witnesses who'd suffered the misfortune of having to play with Douglas during the winter. They were falling over themselves to stand up in court and describe him as an arse of the highest order, his guilt was as clear as the prodigious nose on my face.

Not that I'd initiated any of this nonsense, it was all Douglas's doing. The opening salvo in the litigation process had been the letter I'd received from his solicitor, he'd started it. If only I hadn't capitulated to his lawyer's written demand that I print a letter of apology, conceding a level of guilt where none existed, but it had been traumatic receiving an aggressive solicitor's letter and I'd felt pressured into apologising. I bitterly regretted caving in like that and, after licking my wounds, resolved not to be pushed around by Douglas anymore. Who did he think he was? No, I'd not be browbeaten, his brief could submit wax sealed letters from an ivory tower twice a day for all I cared, it wouldn't stop me continuing to publish fulsome accounts of Douglas's shoddy behaviour for the duration of the tournament. This I did and after a period of silence, during which I assumed Douglas had in fact dropped the matter, I received another letter –

Dear Mr Russon

Despite previous requests for you to remove defamatory material against our client Keith Douglas, we note, with disappointment, that you have failed to comply. We insisted in the strongest possible terms that you remove your insulting descriptions of our client from your blog, yet you have refused so to do. We are therefore left with no alternative but to apply to Aberdeen Sheriff Court insisting action is taken against you for deformation of character. We will naturally be applying for damages to compensate our client's loss of standing in the community.

Yours sincerely

B. Hind Barrs Solicitors

My father brought me up to face bullies head on, not to give in to them, and after I'd relented following the last letter, I resolved that I wouldn't do so again. Instead, I'd give two fingers to Douglas and his over zealous solicitor, they could bog off as far as I was concerned, no-one pushes me around and gets away with it. I appointed a lawyer of my own, G Seeley of No Win No Fee Solicitors Limited, a company I'd seen advertise during a Jeremy Kyle Show commercial break, and looked forward to contesting Douglas in court. I'm not daft, I know when I'm onto a winner, the whole world could see I had no case to answer.

Further correspondence between our respective solicitors followed during the next few weeks including confirmation that Douglas not only wanted compensation, but also reimbursement of his legal costs. The downright cheek, he takes me to court and I've to pay him for the privilege? Er, I don't think so. My solicitor suggested it'd be prudent for me to take a break from writing about him on my Stoney Baloney blog but I felt this would be an admission of guilt, so continued in the same vein. The winter league had long since ended but I was still bumping into the obnoxious wassock. One afternoon in particular, I passed him on the clubhouse steps –

'Russon', he said by way of reluctant acknowledgement.

'What do you want Douglas' I replied.

'Your arse handed tae ye' he grunted, 'and it winna be long now til it is yer f*cking chump.'

'As if any judge will listen to your garbage Douglas, you're full of it. I hope for your sake you pick the right numbers this Saturday evening, you'll need the money to pay for this farce you tosser.'

'Go f*ck yourself Russon' he responded.

'Up yer arse' said I before opening the clubhouse door to escape from the snivelling joker.

We caught sight of each other a couple more times over coming weeks, at Aberdeen Sheriff Court during the opening hearings. On the second occasion, Douglas making a complete idiot of himself...

I pulled up in the Sheriff Court car park half an hour before the hearing and remained in the car to read my newspaper, I enjoy the Sun's Agony Aunt and needed to keep abreast of her ongoing advice to an elderly reader with piles. Twenty minutes later, fully appraised of nature's cruelty in the shape of haemorrhoids, I attempted to vacate my car, just as a van sped into the parking space alongside, leaving insufficient distance for me to open my door. I looked at the driver to find it was none other than Keith flamin' Douglas.

Parking spaces were at a premium, so he'd crammed his oversized van into a tiny opening adjacent to my car, literally leaving no room for either of us to open our driver's doors. I signalled for him to move his van forward but he refused, the stubborn mule, waving his arms around, gesturing for me to move my car instead, a non-starter given I'd parked first and had every right to remain in situe. After further remonstrations it became clear that he wasn't going to cooperate, we'd reached an impasse, neither of us prepared to budge. Eventually, we wound down our windows to discuss the matter, our eyes meeting from a distance of no more than a yard.

'Move your motor Douglas, you moron' I demanded.

'You move yours Russon'

'Bollocks, I was here first'

'Aye but ye hud yer engine on,' he muttered.

'What's that got to do with it?'

'I turned my engine off before you did so I was parked before you were' he grinned. 'Move yourself.'

'I've been sat here for half an hour Douglas, you only just turned up' I replied, somewhat irked.

'I see that Russon, busy studying a pair of women's breasts I notice' he grinned. (My Sun newspaper had fallen open at an inopportune page).

'We're not all as tawdry as you Douglas, I was doing the crossword as a matter of fact.'

'Aye, let me guess, what word has four letters, starts with T and rhymes with 'bits' he sniggered.

'Very funny Douglas, you couldn't spell crossword never mind complete one, now just shift your arse so I can get into court. My solicitor's waiting to tear you a new one.'

By now a handful of our friends had arrived and were looking on, half in interest, half in despair.

'If you don't move that pile of crap Douglas, I'll stick it right up your arse.'

'More threats is it? Hud on while I make a wee note for my solicitor, he'll be pleased to learn the latest if I could only get into the courtroom to speak with him. Shift yersel Russon' bellowed an increasingly smug Douglas, his elbow resting on his opened window, his cheap earring glistening in the sun. 'Shift your poxy car and let's get in there.'

'Shift yours. I was here first.'

'I'll get oot when I'm good and riddy, after you've moved you fat pr*ck.'

The throng of spectators had grown by now, our raised

159

voices persuading bystanders that this was a drama worth investigating. Around a dozen stood gawping at us, some with arms folded, others with hands in their pockets, all with smirks on their faces. My brother Stu was there and shouted across the car park to inform me another space had become vacant. But I wasn't shifting.

'Space for you there Douglas' I said, eye balling the gormless twonk.

'Wouldn't dream of denying you that location Russon, it's in shade, where you spent the entire winter league you f*cking hacker.'

'I was in the shade?! You're off your rocker, you barely strung two pars together Douglas, the only time you did was when I'd already nailed the birdie anyhow, so don't start your crap.'

'You couldn't hit a cow's arse with a banjo,' replied Douglas, 'for the last time, I carried you all through the winter and don't deny it. Your golf's crap, your clothes are crap and your parking's crap. You're a joke min.'

There then followed a most unpleasant exchange of views which resulted in the courthouse security officers called to separate the pair of us, I'd climbed out of my window into Douglas's cab to try and teach him a lesson I'd learned a few years ago on the way home from The White Swan in Erdington. It involved a broken nose and a cauliflower ear. Douglas in turn had me in a headlock, his brother trying to prise me from his clutches before he crashed my head against the dashboard.

'Now now ladies,' sighed the burly security guards, reaching in to drag the pair of us out of the vehicle. 'You'll smudge your lipstick.'

Moments later we were frogmarched into court for a brief hearing and ordered to return for the final decision six weeks hence. I returned to my car afterwards to find Douglas had already gone but my motor had been keyed from boot to bonnet. There could be no doubt who was responsible. How I hated that man.

The six weeks ticked by and we were back at Aberdeen Sheriff Court before we knew it, Douglas standing before the judge in a cheap shellsuit while I'd had the decency to sport a three piece Ralph Lauren number with accompanying sober tie. Our clothes alone told the story, if the decision were based on dress sense, I'd win hands down. The judge looked over his glasses at the pair of us once the usher had asked the courtroom to fall silent, and delivered the following verdict –

> This is without doubt the most futile case I have ever had the misfortune to preside over. Two grown men, Alexander Russon and Keith Douglas, former friends but now sworn enemies, feuding like schoolboys in a playground, all in the name of golf, a pastime I happen to treasure. It is a great disappointment to me that you have sullied the good reputation of our national sport and I only hope the sentence I'm about to hand down ensures there'll be no repeat of such imbecilic behaviour.
>
> It is my duty to address the facts and the facts are these; that Alexander Russon (the defender) did defame Keith Douglas (the pursuer) over a sustained period of time with unsubstantiated allegations which challenged Mr Douglas's honour, golfing ability, personal habits and

freshness of breath. It is my responsibility to decide whether the defender's actions were a) wrong, b) wilful and c) intended to harm. I will provide both parties with written confirmation of my decision however for the time being I would invite you Mr Russon to please stand.

I rose to my feet, placed my hands behind my back and looked forward expectantly. Douglas was smirking, an expression surely to be replaced within the next sixty seconds by one of despair. If I could have recorded footage I would have, but cameras were banned from the court, I'd just have to commit the beauty of this moment to memory and revisit it in the years to come. This was it, this was my time, Douglas was going down and if there was any justice in the world, he'd soon be eating porridge for wasting the court's time, embarking on a five stretch.

Inexplicably however, the judge had other ideas.

Alexander Russon, I find you guilty on all counts brought by the pursuer, Mr Keith Douglas. I am satisfied that the allegations you made against him on your blog *'Stoney Baloney',* were totally without foundation and completely inaccurate. You were invited to withdraw your comments and offer an unreserved apology but failed to do so, offering instead a half-hearted withdrawal which you retracted within days. You then proceeded to repeat these allegations and introduce new ones, thereby cocking a snook at legal protocol.

I am grateful to the Secretary of Stonehaven Golf Club for producing statistical records of your winter league partnership with Keith Douglas in which the facts speak for themselves. Your suggestion that Douglas contributed little was proven to be utter bunkum, let the record show that of the 180 qualifying holes played, you contributed to 17 and Mr Douglas 163. While you claimed to have scored 46 birdies you in fact managed a paltry 5, each of them on Stonehaven's 'gimme' birdie holes. In the final, which your partner effectively qualified your team for singlehandedly, your performance was nothing short of lamentable and only the ability of Mr Douglas carried your partnership to the runners-up spot. I have consulted expert witnesses who played with you during the winter season and they confirm, and I quote, that you were 'inept, hapless and abominable'. Moreover, your accusation that Mr Douglas had halitosis is not only proven unfounded, but witnesses testify to your own personal hygiene being questionable with 'honking oxsters' and 'bison breath that could peel potatoes'. I have no hesitation in supporting Mr Douglas's case against you and it is the order of the court that you pay damages to the tune of £100,000 for the loss of his reputation in the community. In addition I order you to pay the legal costs he has had to incur in bringing this action against you. Get out of my courtroom.

I must concede this all came as rather a shock. My solicitor hadn't turned up, he'd missed his bus from Glasgow, but had reassured me that my case was solid, yet here I was saddled with £200,000 worth of damages and fees, it was quite a surprise

I can tell you. I'd have trouble paying this given my personal 'wealth' totalled zero. Our house was rented not owned, I had no savings and the only cash knocking around the house was our kids' dinner money. How on earth had Douglas managed to win despite all of the promises I'd been made by my solicitor? The advert on his website had said he was yet to lose a case, this I later found out was because he'd never yet contested a case, the bloke was a charlatan, away with the fairies, living a life pretending to be a solicitor until the last moment of a case at which point he'd pull out never to be seen again. I'd been turned over.

The bailiffs came round to my house demanding the money, I told them to sling their hook, they returned with a heavy mob and turfed me out along with my wife and three children. I hadn't been entirely honest with my family about the court proceedings, I didn't want to worry them. Naturally my wife didn't appreciate my explanation and decided to desert me, returning to Birmingham, leaving me to sleep on a park bench down at Mineralwell. It wasn't all bad, I got to keep my CD's after the bailiffs took everything else including, ironically, my golf clubs. You have to laugh.

* * *

Living at Mineralwell was no picnic with foxes nibbling my toes overnight and dogs cocking their legs upon me as I slept. I'd been sacked from my job having brought the name of the company into disrepute and my wordly possessions had been auctioned off to contribute towards Douglas's 'reputational damages' (which stuck in the craw to say the least, his reputation lower than a snake's undercarriage, fifty pence should have covered it never mind a hundred grand). Anyhow, I found some part-time work to keep the wolf from the door, or the fox from my toes. A local joiner had come into a few quid recently and had always wanted a chauffeur, a random personal ambition he'd harboured since school age, a vanity thing to compensate for low self esteem. He wanted someone unknown to him so the arrangement could be kept under the radar, he was fearful his friends would think he'd be giving it the big one if they found out he had a driver. I heard of the job through a recruitment agency and when they told me who the employer was I couldn't resist applying, but knew I'd have to protect my identity. I grew long hair, wore sunglasses and lost four stone in weight to finish off the disguise. My plan was to spend a few months in the job, earn a few quid, then drop my employer in the River Dee while he wore concrete slippers. The employer's name? Douglas, Keith Douglas.

CHAPTER THIRTY ONE

'You're a tragedy starting to happen'
Elbow

With the Winter League now a matter of history, it was time for a fresh challenge, so I set my sights on the Stonehaven Club Championship. The lifting of this trophy would be a fitting accolade, marking the thirtieth anniversary of my Junior Championship victory in 1986. Back then, I brushed the field aside before defeating Frank McCarron in an eighteen hole playoff, this time I planned to make shorter work of my success and have the tournament done and dusted within four rounds, no messing. The committee had other ideas, pressuring me to fix a playoff in their flagship event in an effort to generate additional bar sales from the crowds of spectators who'd inevitably attend the shootout. I kinda understood where they were coming from, although it was rather a tawdry initiative, however I declined when they bolted on a clause waiving my right to an appearance fee.

You have to earn the club championship, no-one gifts it to you, and to this end I commenced a carefully prepared warm up schedule. (By the way, I wasn't mucking around, I was taking on the scratch championship not the second rate handicap division, just plain full on barefoot golf). I'd welcome all-comers; former champions, the current champion, young bucks thinking they were Billy Bigtime, anyone brave enough to have a go if they thought they were hard enough. And those buckling at the knees with news of my participation could thank Craig McKechnie. I was quite content nominating the RBS Pairs title as my next trophy target but our entry to the competition was refused after McKechnie turned up at the club to put our names on the board only to get p*ssed instead and miss the deadline.

My approach would be to cultivate my game upon various courses in the region rather than mindlessly pound balls on a driving range. My agent arranged tee-times at Forfar, Meldrum House, Muirfield and Auchenblae, and that was just for starters. I'd also be participating in minor Stonehaven Golf Club competitions to stir my competitive juices ahead of June's main event (eg. Texas Scramble, 2 Clubs & A Putter, 'Lads On The Lash' outing to Camperdown) but I promised myself not to overdo it.

Round 1 of my preparatory regime was undertaken at Forfar Golf Club alongside a couple of business associates (one of whom signed me in for twelve quid, pretty good deal that). A slightly shaky start saw me open with the number of the beast, 6,6,6, double bogeying each of the first three holes. (I'd had a large lunch in Aberdeen and got stuck in traffic so sprinted onto the first tee which was not ideal. A quick handshake, how do you do, and wallop, away we went, my mind still on the A90). I ripped the last eight holes apart to end with a creditable 84 including a glorious birdie on 11. Agreed, there was room for improvement, but my 84 on a still, dry day off the yellows at a benign Forfar Golf Club would surely strike fear into the hearts of pretenders to this year's Stoney crown. Next stop would be Auchenblae's nine holer on Tuesday night where I would of course, ahem, pay my dues in the honesty box sat next to the unmanned starter's hut.

My physiotherapist had effectively given up on my ailing back, but didn't have the courage to admit it. Instead, she piled up the goose chases, the latest of which was to advise cognitive therapy, my back pain might be in my head she said, the messages my brain sent to my lower back, or vice versa, can't remember which, were perhaps magnifying any perceived pain. She reckoned I'd trained my mind to expect pain, it looked out for it, and when it appeared my brain told me it was more intense than was the actuality. I watched a video presentation by an Australian professor who described in detail the relationship between brain signals and nerve endings, apparently we choose to select a voracity of pain depending on the situation we're in. Stubbing your toe, for example, as you enter the house after a rotten day at work, is more painful than stubbing it on the steps as you embark on a flight to your jollies in Torremolinos. You dwell on the pain caused by the former but brush off the inconvenience of the latter. Fair point, so I decided to take this concept onto the golf course. It lasted thirty seconds, although I'm not sure I was entirely committed.

Usually my lower back pain goes through phases as I swing the club, starting with a dull ache, graduating to a sharp twinge in the backswing and reaching a crescendo of minor agonies upon impact, the swing follow through equally traumatic. Today though I silently repeated a mantra to convince myself that this would not hurt, this would not hurt, this would not hurt. I'm not sure my heart was in it to be frank, but repeating the phrase was at least some sort of concession to my physio and her Australian Professor, after all, I'd tried everything else without there being any signs of improvement. Before swinging the club, I implored my brain not to sense any pain and my lower back not to send any signals to that effect, although I was still confused as to which part of my body was sending signals and which part was deciphering them. In hope rather than expectation, I took the club back, brought it down again and before finishing my swing, cramped up in a convulsion of bloody agony. Believe me, mantra chanting is not all it's cracked up to be, I couldn't even look up to see where the ball went it was so blinking painful. I tried a couple more times but there was no improvement, Lorimer could do one, it was back to the drawing board.

Or should I say back to the physio. I returned to her the following week and shared my golf experience. I'd not given it long enough she claimed, fair enough I suppose, but another element now needed to be brought in from a psychological perspective, according to her, in an effort to distract my mind from a) the pain and b) the overemphasis I'd been placing on golf in my life. Her attitude was that I'd set myself up for a fall, I'd convinced myself that I couldn't cope without golf, it's exclusion would decimate my week, I had nothing else to focus on, I'd built it up as some sort of idol. I needed to reduce the importance I put on golf, she said, and turn my attention to other endeavours, cooking or jigsaws for example. If I told my brain that golf wasn't critical, it would take attention off my back pain because my back pain was telling me I couldn't play golf. Or something like that. So, always one to embrace new ideas, the following day I made the family a beef cobbler and started a thousand piece puzzle of a Mediterranean beach. That night I still went to bed with a sore back, this time achieving only three hours sleep having stayed up until the small hours after a marathon jigsaw session, and in the morning the family took turns on the toilet because I'd not cooked the beef properly. Back, once again, to the drawing board.

She's probably right about golf being too high a priority in my life, but that's the way it is I'm afraid. I'm too old for football, too out of shape for running and not interested in much else. It's a good walk in the fresh air at the very least, even if you're playing like a camel, and if you're playing well it's tremendously rewarding. No, golf would remain in its rightful place at the summit of my extra curricular activities and nothing was gonna stop me. My physio and doctor would just have to do what they were paid to do and find a remedy. Stretches and exercises hadn't worked, nor had manipulation, acupuncture, painkillers, anal investigation, cognotive therapy, cooking and jigsaw puzzles. So I fixed yet another appointment with the quack and he booked me in for an MRI scan to see if there was anything structurally wrong with this back of mine. It was set for three weeks hence.

* * *

The MRI scan didn't come without drama either, my surgical gown opening to reveal my furniture to the radiographer. She hadn't told me I could leave my pants on. The scan results would take a week I was informed, meantime, I'd start a rehabilitation programme set by my physio who'd wangled a free four week membership at the Nuffield Gym. This would provide an opportunity to keep my back joints loose, she said, while boosting my mental state.

It was a posh gym, a million miles from the council run one I frequented in Walsall, where folk stood outside smoking, litter blocked the entrance and graffiti covered the walls. No this one attracted business types, the annual fee covered by employers as part of a remunerative package. The facility straddled three floors; the changing rooms and swimming pool at the basement, reception and cafeteria on the ground floor, weights and cardio machines on the top. Members taking the elevator to the gym up above really needed to consider their commitment if they couldn't shift their fat arses up two flights of stairs for a work out.

I wasn't exercising to lose three stone and clinch a modelling contract, I was there to keep my back supple and create a sense of overall mental wellbeing, nevertheless, it's chastening to enter a changing room littered with bulging biceps and tanned skin when you've got a physique like Christopher Biggins. I carry fifteen stones of blubber, boasting a wobbly blancmange of a midriff beneath an unsightly moob mountain, so I threw my gear on sharpish and scurried off to evacuate my bowels before getting into the lift.

Once in the gym, six pounds lighter, I spent half an hour on a cross trainer positioned before two flat screens which broadcasted Jeremy Kyle (screen 1) and Sky Sports (screen 2). Ordinarily there'd be no contest for my attention, but with Kyle's topic being 'My Mother Stole My Boyfriend', Kirsty Gallagher would have to wait. After thirty minutes of exercise I visited the stretching zone to do 'the plank', a static stretch in the press up position aimed at strengthening the base of your spine. Unfortunately however, my back was so weak that I was shuddering like a sh*tting puppy after ten seconds so had to pack it in and return to cardio work for five more minutes before calling the session quits.

Returning to the changing rooms, 1 stripped naked and caught a glimpse of myself in the mirror. My word I was out of shape, a grotesque wobble fest of palid lard, a sobering sight. I wrapped a towel around my girth to conceal my glory but did so too tightly, my moobs now even more prominent, hanging forlornly over the towel band. I know I'm not built like a brick outhouse or likely to be nominated as the next Bond , but the rolls of flab crowning my hips and puffy man breasts were horrific confirmation that I needed to get in shape if I was to win this golf championship. It now dawned on me that a diet of pies, chips and puddings was not the way forward, strapping myself in every teatime for mammoth belch inducing, bowel busting festivals of food was no longer acceptable. This visit to the gym had fortified my resolve to get in shape, a sensible diet alongside a ten week fitness regime would have me turning up on the first tee for the championship's opening round looking like a Greek God. Lack of practice wasn't an issue, class is permanent and I'd turn the birdies on like a tap, I just needed to ensure my fitness was such that I could complete the 72 holes. I'd start in earnest tomorrow (after I'd watched the football and polished off tonight's Indian).

CHAPTER THIRTY TWO

'You would not think to look at him that he was famous long ago'
Bob Dylan

The place I'd spend my dying day, whatever the weather, and I'm pretty sure it would be raining, is Stonehaven Golf Club. If Stonehaven is the place I call home then its golf course is, and forgive the impertinence of adopting a colloquial Scottish term, 'ma scratcher'. I've spent countless hours on that piece of land, all of them happy ones. The exposed nature of the course, overhanging the north sea, unprotected from the elements, has you facing testing conditions whatever the time of year and it isn't unusual to experience all fours seasons in one day. Apart perhaps from the young trees in the 'field' (holes 9-12) there's nowhere to hide should the heavens open and no trees to shield you from the howling wind, this is golf at the sharp end. The terrain, lying alongside the cliff's edge, is severely undulated with humps and hollows, valleys and climbs. There's no other golf course like it. It doesn't rank amongst many people's favourite golf courses, but to a twelve year old boy taking up golf for the first time it was all I knew and I've loved it ever since.

Stonehaven golf course is not your slash and burn track, strategic placement is the name of the game. You could comfortably play it with a set of irons and have equal success as someone booming drives off every tee. There's trouble everywhere. Take your pick from slicing out of bounds on 2,3 or 7, hooking or pushing it onto the railway at 9,10,16 or 17 and that's before we speak of the fabled 'gully', a three hole test of nerve requiring straight and solid striking, or oblivion. The course is very well groomed, so while the climate and terrain might be held up as an excuse for poor scoring, the quality of the greens cannot. I played here for four glorious years before returning to Birmingham in '86, shortly after winning the Junior Championship. Oh, hadn't I mentioned my championship victory? Well let's put that straight.

(Plumps up cushions, reclines in chair, puffs out chest...)

It was the summer of 1986, a hot sun baking the greens, the fairways veritable runway strips. Half a dozen teenage members began the fourth and final round of the Stonehaven Junior Championship, each with a genuine chance of glory. I held a narrow lead over Douglas, Ross, Ferguson, Innes and McCarron, there may have been others but memory fails me, no obvious winner presented himself. With two holes to play, word had reached me (falsely) that I was at least three shots ahead and needed only to keep my nose clean for guaranteed golfing glory. So when I drained a birdie putt on the 17th I felt I had sufficient breathing space to stink out the 18th and still win. I was rehearsing my winner's speech as I stood on the final tee, waiting for the green to clear, watching Frank McCarron line up a monster putt from the back of the green. I looked on impassively as he holed his lengthy attempt, but was puzzled by his elaborate celebration, charging around the green's perimeter, punching the air, clenching his fists Seve style and offering high fives to playing partners. Why was he so ecstatic? My calculations reckoned he'd need to have carded a 67 to beat me, yet none of us had broken 70 in the thousands of rounds of golf we'd played in recent years. I ruled out his assumption of victory, assuming news had falsely filtered back to him that his co-leaders had all shot their bolt, and continued about my business. I teed off, pushing it upon the slope before the first tee, chipped down to twenty feet and nonchalantly two putted before hauling my way up the hill to the waiting crowds (okay, sprinkling of people).

'75?' I said to my brother Stu, enquiring politely whether this was sufficient for victory, expecting a prompt endorsement. Those around him scurried off to report my score and returned excitedly to announce that I had tied with Frank, he had indeed shot a 67, including a birdie two on the last. We were to alight three days later for an eighteen hole play-off.

The play-off started in controversy. I've never had a caddy before or since, but my mate Jason had volunteered and I'd accepted. Frank was unhappy about this (rightly, looking back) believing it to be an unfair advantage, not so much because I'd be fresher but because I'd have a cheerleader by my side while he trudged along alone. Frank's father had driven him up to the course so calmed choppy waters by agreeing to caddy for his son. If I had my time again I'd do the honourable thing and drop the caddy, but when you're sixteen and your best mate offers to be part of your big moment you lose all sense of decency. Jason had never seen me play golf and while he was the local hero, being lead singer in a band, my identity was as a 'hanger-on' so it puffed me up to think I could take centre stage before him, if only for a day.

The first two holes defined the play-off. Two nervous golfers hacking their way down the opening hole and walking off the green with triple bogey sevens. Frank sliced his tee shot out of bounds, I thundered my second shot through the green and down the cliffs, nerves were surely jangling. The second hole though, left Frank with a mountain to climb. I blasted a straight tee shot to the fringe, chipped on and holed for a three while Frank sliced two balls out of bounds and slunk off the green with a quadruple bogey seven. A four shot lead after two holes, despite starting the round with a seven, gave me confidence to go on and win the trophy, though in rather understated fashion, the midweek fixture attracting a crowd of zero and I was welcomed back into the clubhouse by a solitary fellow, Jim, from whom I ordered a pie and beans. Alex Russon, Junior Champion 1986. Have it.

CHAPTER THIRTY THREE

'This is the end, I'll say goodbye, the final curtain'
The Charlatans

Sadly, the story now takes a pitiful turn, which I take no pride in telling. Desperate people do desperate things and I regrettably joined the ranks of miscreants who have sullied the name of their sport, something I'll have to live with for the rest of my life.

The Russon v Douglas court case had cost me dear. I'd been stripped of every penny I possessed, wound up kipping on a park bench and my wife had left me. She'd pleaded with me not to risk the family silver, to settle the dispute with Douglas out of court, but I was determined to defend my family's name against his belligerent bullying. In the event, an inept defender of the crown had ruled against me so I faced a very unhappy future unless I could devise a way of recouping the huge financial losses and atone for the misery I'd caused my family. Perhaps then they'd return to my bosom, my ample moob-mountain of a bosom, and we'd all live happily ever after. So I hatched a plan.

The first three rounds of the club championship had not gone well. I sat fully twenty six shots behind the leader as we entered the final 18 holes, indeed of all the entrants to the scratch division, I lay last, six shots behind the nearest competitor. The field hadn't so much crept away from me as sprinted full tilt over the horizon. My continued involvement seemed futile, however, I had good reason to see it through.

My children were virtually estranged from me and it hurt like hell. So disgusted was their mother with their father that she'd returned to Walsall and I now saw the kids only occasionally. I couldn't afford the travel south and had nowhere to accommodate them if they visited me, so my mother rustled up the cash to pay for me to take the train down to Birmingham a couple of times and shack up in a Travelodge. This was both painful and humiliating, you want your kids to be proud of you not bewildered as to why their father, who once tucked you up in bed at night, was now absent for six week intervals and sleeping rough in the park you used to frequent with your friends. I hoped that winning the Stonehaven Championship would return some of the pride they once had in me and if the cunning plan I'd devised to recoup the money succeeded, I could return them and their mother to the lifestyle to which they'd become accustomed.

Perversely, the distance I found myself behind the leader of the championship was a blessing. The bookmakers in the town liked to provide odds on who'd lift the trophy, something of a tradition started fifty years ago by a bookie who was also a member of the club. My odds had plummeted to 150-1 and while being a damned cheek, gave rise to the potential of a nice little earner. 150-1! Blimey, if I put just a tenner on myself and won, that'd be fifteen hundred nicker. And if I put a hundred quid on I'd win fifteen grand, a very welcome boost to my finances, providing the opportunity to visit the children rather more often. But hold on, imagine if I found ten grand in stake money and won the tournament? That would be a million and a half quid's worth of winnings, now you were talking life changing money, getting a massive house type money, reuniting your family and making your kids proud again sort of money. The trauma of the last year would be a distant dream, we could stride forward together with a skip in our step as if the whole episode had never happened. My wife could kick with the fray, the children could be educated at Lathallan and never mind me being a chauffeur, I could employ one myself. I'd have him park my Bentley directly outside Douglas's house every single night as a permanent reminder as to who really was the Daddy in town. Every dog has his day and this was going to be mine, I just needed to find ten grand... and win the tournament.

Finding the cash was the easy part. Well let's face it, I work for a bank and you don't look a gift horse in the mouth. The financial sector had been under intense scrutiny for several years and as a result, miles of red tape and encyclopaedic length books of compliance were devoted to protecting the public's money. It was harder than ever for tricksters to appropriate funds illegally, however, they still found a way, and if they could do it from the outside I was damned sure I could from the inside. I wasn't going to overlook this golden opportunity to wet my beak. What harm would a couple of quid cause anyhow? I wasn't going to give it the full Nick Leeson and break the bank, just dip in for a spot of loose change and moreover, I'd pay it back once the bookie coughed up my winnings. No harm done, a victimless crime.

So on the Saturday afternoon, an hour or so after completing a lamentable 76 to place me twenty six shots behind tournament leader Roger Smith, I took a trip to my employer's office in Aberdeen. Aside from Shirley, the friendly security guard, there was no one around and after I'd fooled her with some patter about collecting a file while shopping in town, she granted me entry to the second floor where I made myself comfortable in front of a computer terminal. Three minutes later and I was looking at Keith Douglas's business account, it made interesting reading. Amounts were leaving the account to various websites including 'Whip Me & Spank Me Big Boy' and ' Enter A Sheep Here' which may have been a site for the farming community to register livestock, but may not. And what was this? A huge entry into the account from LA Casinos Online, one hundred and seventy five grand! I was well aware of his penchant for casinos and the success he'd had in this regard but Gordon Bennet, that was a huge windfall. His account boasted a balance of nearly a quarter of a million quid! In a fit of peek, persuaded by a combination of envy and greed, I impulsively transferred to my account not the ten grand I'd planned, but a hundred grand. This would be my stake.

Bank systems don't allow staff access to online betting shops so I now had to walk to the library down the road where I logged into my bank account. There sat a balance of £95,107 (I'd been nearly five thousand overdrawn prior to the cash transfer). In a flash, before allowing time to change my mind, I bet the whole lot on myself to win the Stonehaven Club Championship, at 150-1. It's amazing how many betting sites will give odds on scenarios you'd assume they'd have no intelligence on, word surely travels fast in their world, bookmakers sharing information as they spread their risk. Either that or they'd sneaked a look at the leaderboard and written me off to such an extent that they thought I was toast, but these people had not reckoned on the next part of my plan.

Recovering from a twenty six shot deficit appeared absolutely impossible. Given the leader hadn't scored worse than 72 in several years, I estimated that I would need to card something in the order of a 46 simply to tie, quite a feat given the course record was 60. It was clear that other steps needed to be taken to eliminate Mr Smith from contention, and here I had a couple of options open to me. The first, a bullet in the head from point blank range, this appeared a little heavy handed so I plumped for option two, a liberal dose of laxatives in his traditional pre-match coffee. He'd be decimating trap one when called to the first tee and be disqualified for not turning up on time. I knew a chemist who'd help me select a suitably fearsome, bog busting laxative to have him seated on the throne for hours, while I was out on the course winning the tournament.

Ridding the leaderboard of Smith's name was relatively simple, the real conundrum came in eliminating the remainder of the field. I could only rely upon Smith to take the bait, his routine drinking of coffee before every game was legendary, but I didn't know what the rest of the leaders did before play so alternative plans needed to be laid. A swift brainstorm provided no nuggets, only fanciful dreams that belonged in Disneyland; training rabbits to steal golf balls from the fairway, placing cling film over the holes after I'd putted out, tampering with each completed scorecard but my own, super gluing flagsticks for unsuspecting competitors to attach themselves to when attending the pin, electrifying pathways, the list went on. But then came my eureka moment.

A customer of mine in Portlethen had recently introduced a ground breaking product which was already in great demand by the oil and gas industry. With modern technology developing at breakneck speed, never a day went by without another launch or invention and he'd designed a device that the industry was gagging for, giving companies the ability to identify defects in both subsea and overhead constructions, which in turn enabled a prompt repair thereby avoiding long term damage. Called 'The Spotter', it was an aerial drone which could be operated by a landlubber from the comfort of his office, rather like a deluxe remote controlled helicopter. Say there was concern over the extent of damage to equipment stowed high on an oil platform out in the North Sea, rather than send a poor lackey to climb up the shaky scaffolding and inspect said problem, a simple reconnaissance exercise using The Spotter would reveal all, without putting human life in danger. The drone was barely the size of an apple, yet could be operated from a distance of five thousand yards, like a puppet on a string. Ingenious. I remembered asking him which other industries his product might be useful for and he'd explained there was nothing to prevent it being used for a myriad of purposes, the technology was developed, it was simply a case of marketing the concept. A tiny reader was inserted into a spherical object and received messages from a handheld device orchestrating its journey. The camera element, while critical to most adaptations, wasn't obligatory, occasionally The Spotter was sent up purely to record sound or could in fact be used as a missile, although permission had yet to be granted in this regard. The Scottish government was not yet ready to sanction surface to air missiles from a lockup in Portlethen.

My idea was this; if I could persuade, or let's face it, bribe Derek, to adapt his drone in such a fashion that it could work within a golf ball, and be directed around a golf course remotely, I might have something to work with. Initially he seemed doubtful, but I reminded him of his entrepreneurial spirit, his product might open the floodgates to new markets, plus I knew about his affair with the company receptionist and wondered if his wife might like me to share the news. I explained what I planned to use 'The Spotter' for, as a tool to demonstrate to budding young golfers what the perfect trajectory of a golf ball should be. I confessed that I couldn't replicate the perfect flight every time I hit the ball, although I could on the great majority of cases, and a device like this provided a continuous repetition which illustrated to golfers how a ball should arc in its travel. His eyes lit up. He was in.

* * *

Show me an eight year old who isn't a wizard with a tablet, iPhone, Kindle or equivalent. They're all experts. My son Freddie being no exception, evidence of a misspent youth it might be, but in his case it was a pathway to riches, or strictly speaking, his father's.

Freddie loved golf, so much so that at the tender age of eight he'd already completed several rounds on all of the world's top courses; St. Andrews, Augusta, Pebble Beach, Royals Troon, Birkdale and St. Georges, all courtesy of his faithful Kindle app 'Around The World In 80 Plays'. His scoring was pretty impressive, seldom out of the sixties, and he spent hours trying to better his various course records, making mincemeat of the game's best layouts. He'd had the temerity to break sixty on several tracks and would commonly take no more than twenty four putts in a round. Such proficiency gave rise to boredom however, he'd mastered most courses and needed a fresh challenge to reinvigorate his interest, so I found Stonehaven Golf Club on his app and set him a challenge of breaking 50 (possible given Stoney's standard scratch was only 65). He wanted to impress his father, particularly since we didn't see each other very often

185

nowadays, so committed hours to the project, tirelessly devoting himself to the discovery of every nook and cranny the course possessed. Before long he was routinely scoring in the mid 50's and, but for an unscheduled interruption for a shopping trip with his mother, was three holes from breaking the magic 50 mark.

Meanwhile, Derek was investigating another new product, a hybrid between his Spotter and Freddie's app. How cool would it be, we ruminated, if a golf ball being used in genuine play, could be fitted with one of his drones which in turn was operated via a remote control device connected to an app. In other words, wouldn't it be a thrill if Freddie were able to steer my golf ball around Stonehaven Golf Club from the moment it left the first tee to the second it dropped into the hole on the 18th? " Was this possible?" I enquired of Portlethen's Professor Derek. " Yes it was" came the reply. The right answer.

The day of the final round came, Freddie and I arriving at the golf club an hour or so early, my nerves shredded with the anticipation of what might unfold. Brenda was shuffling around the clubhouse, big smiles as always, otherwise the place was empty. Freddie took a seat next to the window which provided the most spectacular view from any clubhouse I know, an awe inspiring blanket of rolling waves beneath a bright blue summer sky. Today was a scorcher, perfect weather for a sub 60 round.

Leaving Fred to play on his Kindle, I visited the locker room below the clubhouse to prepare for the round of golf that would, hopefully, change my life forever, the forthcoming eighteen holes beckoning a financial windfall and golfing glory. Scoffers belittling my chances after the opening three rounds could sod off, they wouldn't be so patronising come the Autumn when they'd walk, for the umpteenth time, past my name on the championship scroll of honour. And Douglas could bugger off aswell, I'd have the biggest house in Stoney thanks to his unwitting provision of my stake money, oh the sweet irony, he sues my ass off yet funds my future without even knowing it, beautiful. All I needed to do was execute the plan, concentration was key.

Pulling a gleaming golf ball from my pocket, I checked it for the hundredth time, pleading with it to convey authenticity in the hours to come, but concerned that folk might spot the slight difference to a conventional golf ball. This one was slightly oversized with an intermittent, though mercifully slight, flicker of light emanating from within, flashing faintly like a lighthouse through a pea souper of a fog. This was no ordinary golf ball, this was an electronically bugged missile which, upon impact from my golf club, would have its voyage directed by a remote control, operated obliviously, by my son Freddie, seated in the clubhouse. He'd become an expert of Stonehaven Golf Club with his online app and Professor Derek had found a way to link Freddie's online efforts with my golf ball. Provided Fred retained his focus and completed the eighteen holes without interruption, I could guarantee a score in the 50's, possibly better.

The laxatives worked a treat. Poor Smith was defecating through the eye of a needle within seconds of his coffee, he'd barely reached trap one when the world fell out of his bottom. The poor bloke lost half his body weight during the next four hours, the triple helping of 'Laxo+' emptying his pipes and then some. When his playing partners discovered why he wasn't on the tee, an ambulance was called halfway through his mammoth lavatory session, but Smith couldn't stay off the throne long enough to be transferred into the vehicle. Every time he pulled his pants up they were immediately returned to his ankles as he nestled upon the pan for further evacuation. Disappointed though he was to be disqualified from the tournament, his first priority was to rehydrate his body which had become virtual skin and bone, his ring piece shredded to ribbons.

There remained a strong field despite Smith's demise. A dozen or so had been jockeying for position over the first three rounds and seven players lay within four shots of each other. I was the rank outsider being fourteen shots back but now had a secret weapon that would blow them away, I just needed to make it convincing. Freddie's wizardry on the handheld was a given, I just needed to swing the golf club in a convincing enough fashion that the trajectory of the golf ball could be believed. If my swing resembled the amateurish hoick of a three year old child but my golf ball travelled three hundred yards, suspicion would arise. While not exhibiting the swing of a professional, I at least needed to illustrate a motion which deserved the ball's resultant resting place. My golf swing was pretty tidy, that wasn't an issue, but with such a debilitating back injury I worried that a total collapse upon impact might give the game away. I dosed up on Tramadol to ease the pain, a medication ordinarily capable of felling a horse, but my slipped disc was giving me severe gip so I needed something potent.

My start time was in twenty minutes time, at 11.15 precisely, I'd be playing alongside Bruce Ferguson and, just my bleeding luck, Keith bloody Douglas. We'd not played together since our winter league adventure and had vowed never to play together again, but the fixture list was destined to reunite us at some point, we just had to suck it up. It was Bruce I felt sorry for, four hours of tumbleweed ridden silence awaited although this may prove advantageous, allowing him to concentrate fully on his game. Advancing towards the tee, I took a deep breath as the enormity of this life changing round of golf struck me, it felt like it might overwhelm me for a moment or two, until I gathered myself sufficiently to approach my playing partners for the customary handshake.

'Morning Bruce, good to see you,' I ventured, 'brought your A game with you?'

'Yep, no point leaving it at home.' he chuckled, shaking my hand warmly.

I then turned to Keith who was dressed like a Guantanamo Bay detainee and circus clown all rolled into one, head to foot in bright orange with a white cap decorated with small swirly patterns, every colour of the rainbow.

'Playing golf or off for an audition Douglas? You look ridiculous'. I couldn't help myself.

Keith strode towards me, with a face like thunder, coming so close I thought he wanted to kiss me. I was wrong.

'Listen up Russon. I'm haein none o' yer sh#te the day right? Keep oot o' my face or I'll bend 'is club roond yer neck and hang ye fae the railway bridge. Just f#ck off. Right?'

As first tee greetings go I'd had warmer, but his hostility wasn't entirely unexpected. Bruce was smirking, he'd guessed there'd be fireworks and found the opening salvos entertaining, less so however the club captain who'd alighted on the tee to wish all competitors well. He'd learned through the grapevine of our ongoing feud but was taken aback at the vehemence of Douglas's threat.

189

'I don't feel there's any call for that Keith if you don't mind me saying so. We're a friendly club here at Stonehaven. I'd be obliged if you'd shake Mr Russon's hand and apologise.'

My son, Freddie, stood at the window of the clubhouse, waiting for my signal. We'd enjoyed a pleasant meal the night before, well a haggis supper on the beach front, and had a man to man conversation about what we would do if we ran into a fortune. Of course the measurement of richness varies between eight year old boys and middle aged men, to Freddie's mind a hundred quid represented a fortune and, if he ever appropriated such wealth, he planned to blow it on the biggest Lego set in the land.

'Tell you what ' I said, ' let's see if we can make that happen. If I told you Daddy could get you £100 as a prize for playing a computer game, what would you say?'

He looked bemused, the innocent workings of a child's mind whirring away behind those beautiful blue eyes of his. I explained that the creators of his favourite golfing app had launched a competition, players under the age of ten won a hundred quid if they completed a virtual round of golf in no more than fifty shots. The rules were that it had to be played at their local golf club and during the final round of the nominated club's championship. Wide eyed excitement soon gave way to a concentrated, steely gaze.

'I could do that Dad! I've scored fifty on Stonehaven before, no sweat, can I enter? Please?'

'Do you think you can do that Fred? It'd take a lot of concentration.'

'Yeah, honest Dad, I can. Please let me. I could get that Lego kit I've always wanted, you know the one, Star Wars with the whole battlefield and everything. Please!' He was jumping up and down in his chair like an excited cocker spaniel, desperate for his master to give him a treat.

'Well if you really think you can do it Freddie, let's go for it, I'll play the final round tomorrow and you can sit in the clubhouse trying to score the magic fifty, or even beat it!'

That it should come to this, hoodwinking my own son into becoming an accessory to crime, bribing him into action as an unwitting sports cheat. It doesn't get much lower, I'd stooped to the depths. Keith Douglas had a lot to answer for when he met his maker, driving me to such reprehensible lengths of desperation, if it wasn't for his damned lawsuit none of this would ever have happened. He'd get his one day and no mistake.

So there I stood, issuing the pre-arranged thumbs up sign to Freddie, his signal to crank up the Kindle and get himself comfortable, our first shot was imminent. Feeling somewhat panicked, I looked desperately at my golf ball, pleading for a faint flicker to reveal itself from within, a pale flashing light confirming the satellite connection had succeeded and that my ball was now primed for direction from Fred's fair hand. Yes, there it was, mercifully dull so as not to raise suspicion yet comfortingly apparent, the plan remained on track.

I was quaking with trepidation ahead of this opening drive, the moment of truth. If this shot shanked its way to the cemetery I'd know all bets were off, the game was a bogey. I had faith in Freddie's gaming ability, but I feared for the viability of the connection between his device and my ball. Equally, I worried that the critical time delay built in between Freddie's actions and mine might corrupt, the two needed to be entirely in synch otherwise my foot long tap-ins might travel three hundred yards and my drives barely reach the ladies' tees. Derek had assured me that the receiver hidden inside my golf ball had been fitted with a state of the art memory chip that would ensure the ball travelled the appropriate distance and direction, according precisely to Freddie's promptings. My goodness I hoped he was right.

It was time. The captain announced my name, to a gathering crowd of literally no-one, and I shuffled nervously to the tee.

'Have a good game gentlemen' I said, cheerily.

'You too Alex' replied Bruce.

'F*ck off Russon' followed Keith.

Bloody charming.

And with that I drew my club into a creditable backswing, brought it down at sensible pace towards my winking golf ball and followed through while muttering a heartfelt plea for it to travel dead straight for two hundred and eighty yards. It was sh*t or bust time. I closed my eyes virtually tight shut but sneaked a peek at the ball's journey, almost weeping as it soared like an eagle before coming down a matter of feet from the first green. Derek's gizmo had only gone and done it! I could be leaving this course a millionaire.

Nine birdies later, we stood on the tenth tee, my playing partners aghast, they'd never seen anything like it. My every shot had been textbook golf, my ball searing through the skies off the tee, delivered within a dustbin lid of the hole from the fairway and nonchalantly tapped into the cup from never more than two feet. Freddie was on fire. There'd been one slight alarm on the eighth green when Douglas approached my ball believing it to be his own, and remarked upon a flash of light he felt it emitted, but I quickly scurried across to mark it and told him the thing was on fire, no wonder it was giving off light.

'How did yer nae play like 'is in the winter Russon? You were sh#te' he muttered as he totted up my first nine on the scorecard.

'That was my warm up event Douglas, I wasn't gonna waste my fireworks on you was I. You might've peaked, I was just practicing.'

'Hats off to you Alex' said Bruce, in a rather more congratulatory tone than Douglas had mustered, 'fantastic golf, it's like you're playing a different game.'

I looked at him hesitantly, 'playing a different game?' Was this a jibe? Had he clocked me? Was he inferring knowledge of my ruse? No, he couldn't possibly know and if he did they'd have called time on me before now. I addressed my first tee shot of the back nine and duly delivered it three hundred yards up the middle.

Douglas and Bruce were playing respectably themselves but had been rattled by my procession of birdies. Since the fourth or fifth they'd been trying to force the issue, desperate to compete with my scoring, and had taken risks which lead to bogeys. While my score improved, theirs suffered, and into the final few holes of the competition I knew I was in contention. We reached the archway between the twelfth and thirteen holes, three birdies later, and bumped into the final group as they made their way to the ninth tee. With Roger Smith out of the picture, and probably still on the sh#tter, this threeball represented the top of the leaderboard when the final round began and their demeanour suggested as such, focussed, silent, marching resolutely without so much as a 'hello'. They had their game faces on and were escorted by the club captain and a sprinkling of spectators, mostly dutiful family members. Unable to resist, I enquired, on behalf of the also rans, as to who was leading the chase.

'To tell the truth, ah hink a wee bitty 'o nerves has crept in' confided a concerned looking mother. 'They're nae playin weel ken, dinna hink 'ony o' them'll brak sivinty.'

This was music to my ears, but I feigned disappointment. If she was right, I'd win this at a canter, my calculations had allowed for a 63 or worse from the leader if my 50 was to win it, their demise gave me breathing space and if it continued this way, only Douglas could genuinely compete for the title. Miraculously, he'd matched my last three birdies since the 10th and this kept him on course as a serious challenger, although he'd need at least another couple of birdies to beat me.

Standing a few yards away, I overheard Bruce's conversation with the captain, he was exuberantly describing the incredible round I was putting together and El Capitan glanced wide eyed in my direction, granting me a nod of respectful congratulation. Twelve under par for twelve holes was big news indeed, and as he walked away I could see the captain reporting back to base on his walkie talkie, Stonehaven Golf Club likes to keep with tradition, none of your modern day iPhones and the like. There was big news going down here on the back nine and he wanted those in the clubhouse to know it, perhaps a couple more spectators might want to join us, he suggested.

The gully is the stretch of holes between the thirteenth and fifteenth, synonymous with the club, the signature holes in many respects. It's a section of the course where competitions are won and lost, three short holes which can be completed in an aggregate of nine strokes with accurate tee shots, but if you're wayward you'll rack up a cricket score. The drive on the thirteenth requires a carry of a hundred yards, a duff spells curtains, a hook puts you on the train tracks and a slice sends you down the cliffs, there ain't much room for error. The fourteenth is a blind par three, pull your ball left and you sleep with the fishes and the fifteenth hole, back across the gully, gobbles up any short ball. It's a tough run and players need to be on their game to negotiate it. Sadly, Freddie was not on his as I teed off on the gully's opening hole.

Up until now, Fred's ability on that Kindle of his had shone through perfectly. The hundred quid tempter was doing the job, twelve holes and twelve birdies, I couldn't have asked for more. In truth I'd expected the occasional par or even bogey but could never have dreamed he'd perform like this, he was turning me into a legend. But now came his first error, and a costly one. As my drive left the club I knew he'd botched it, he'd tried to drive the green instead of laying up, and the ball flew wildly out of bounds. I could have wrung his neck. Rubbing salt into the wound, Douglas did drive the green before ramming in a raker for an eagle while I reloaded for a double bogey six, a four shot swing providing Douglas with the outright lead. Flippin' 'eck Fred, I needed you to step up to the plate on the next hole son, there was making up to do.

What I hadn't been aware of when the captain had communicated with the clubhouse via his walkie talkie half an hour earlier, was that Willie Donald was on the other end and had shared the exchange with younger members kicking around the club. They in turn had notified social media and the thing had gone viral in the blink of an eye, moreover, anybody residing within a few miles of the club, had descended on the course and was presently lining the final three holes. It was absolutely unheard of for a player of any repute down the ages to score so many consecutive birdies and if history was being made, they wanted to be part of it. I identified with that, when Brian Lara was nearing his world record quadruple hundred for Warwickshire back in the nineties, I was one of the thousands who'd caught wind of it on the radio and raced along to Edgbaston to witness the event. Now it was me that was the big news, me, Alex Russon, recently humbled in the eyes of the community following Douglas's cruel lawsuit, but now destined to be hero of the town if not the country. I'd have a bit of that thank you very much, instant stardom was fine by me. And it appeared to start right here and now, thousands of spectators either side of the fairway forming a tunnel of turf from tee to green, just like on the telly.

I was thirteen under par with three holes to play and about to play an eminently birdieable par five, the 16th. Word now had it that the aforementioned leaders had blown up completely and the only genuine contenders were myself and Douglas, Bruce had played adequately but was too far back to challenge, it was a straight fight. Booming our drives up the middle, we felt like royalty as we were cheered and applauded every step of the way to our respective balls, well I say 'we' but in truth, it was me alone to whom the rapturous reception was directed.

Our behaviour as we advanced along the fairway amidst this surreal atmosphere was an interesting study in the psychological make up of the human mind. Different personalities behave in different ways when faced with an alien situation, Bruce drifted along with a beaming smile on his face, lapping it up, thrilled by an experience he could never have dreamt would happen, soaking himself in the moment even allowing himself the occasional wave to the crowd. Douglas on the other hand was unimpressed, he viewed this as a ludicrous over reaction and a grotesque inconvenience, he was busting a gut to win the championship yet found himself in the middle of a circus. Enraged by the whole affair, he drove the remote controlled trolley that housed his clubs and assortment of ridiculous hats, towards a section of spectators, scattering them onto the fourth fairway as they ran for their lives. Douglas set it to maximum speed as it terrorised screaming members of the general public, kids were crying and mothers shrieking as the damned thing lurched forward after each handbrake turn, accelerating up to speeds of 40mph as it headed for its next victim. Only when a couple of blokes advanced towards Douglas in a somewhat threatening manner did he cool the beans and return his trolley to its intended purpose rather than using it as a lethal weapon. For my part, I approached the occasion with composure and class, I belonged to this environment, it had just taken forty odd years to arrive that's all. Check the scorecard people, then compare it to any scorecard ever compiled in the history of the game, it was unsurpassed, imperious, in one afternoon I'd earned my place not amongst the best in the game but as *the* best in the golfing world. I deserved this acclaim and refused to be phased by it, so strode forward with pride, touching the peak of my cap in acknowledgement of the fevered applause I was receiving every step of the way. Douglas was hating every second of my notoriety, which made it all the sweeter.

We played out the sixteenth, all three of us birdieing the hole with a nonchalance belying the gravity of the occasion, but as we walked to the seventeenth tee, dark clouds began to form overhead. We'd benefitted from unbroken sunshine since we'd set out three hours prior, but a breeze had worked itself up and the sun had disappeared behind the darkening sky, the temperature dropping a few degrees too, people were pulling on sweaters. Back in the clubhouse, Freddie remained rooted to the seat he'd been using since the first tee and continued his sterling job. I reckoned that two more birdies from these final two holes would be enough to beat Douglas, who'd rallied well on the back nine, but surely couldn't keep matching my birdie blitz. Even if he managed one on this short par four, he would surely not follow it up on the two hundred plus yard par three. All I need do was continue swinging the club in the credible fashion I had exhibited thus far and Fred would do the rest. I'd kiss him when I got back to the clubhouse, I might even award him an extra tenner for his efforts.

Spots of rain accompanied our play on the seventeenth and umbrellas popped up among the enthralled spectators, desperate to see if I could complete a round of golf in a world record fifty strokes. By now there were over five thousand people lining the last two holes, standing at every available vantage point; in the car park, in front of the clubhouse, on the first tee, upon the cemetery wall, on car rooftops, some kids had even shimmied up drainpipes to the clubhouse roof, others were perched on the fencing around the third tee, they were everywhere, eager to witness history in the making. The spots of rain as we teed off didn't interfere with proceedings despite becoming gradually heavier as the three of us took our turn, Bruce sliding his up the middle while Douglas and I drifted slightly left. With much whooping and hollering from the crowds, we marched on, Douglas still sailing close to the wind with the proximity of his speeding trolley to the watching gallery.

'Take it easy Douglas, you're gonna kneecap someone with that bloody thing' I ventured.

'F*ck-all to do wi' you Russon' came the curt reply.

'Just turn the speed down a notch before you run some poor kid over.'

'Mind your own business' he responded, in no mood to tame his behaviour, remote control fixed firmly in his right hand as he shoved it in my face. 'And another 'hing Russon' he hissed from a distance of barely a yard, 'I dinna ken fit yer up to and how you've done 'it, but this hale thing today stinks. There's no way on earth you could score this well, but I'll find oot fit wy you've done it and you'll be finished.'

'You'll need to brush up on that runners up speech of yours Douglas' I responded, 'too many sour grapes in that one.'

'Boll#cks. You play like a complete airse for a full winter then I'm expected to swallow this? You're a f*cking cheat.'

'Prove it Douglas' I said as we eyeballed each other. 'Look around you, there's five thousand witnesses watching me grind you into the dirt. Man up you waster. I'm beating you, fair and square or otherwise you're going down, button your cakehole and deal with it.'

We'd reached our respective golf balls and turned our thoughts to finding the green with our approach shots. The sky continued to darken and a faint roll of thunder could be heard as several more umbrellas went up. We carried on regardless, Bruce stiffing his pitch to two feet while Keith and I found the centre of the green which by the time we reached it, had been drenched by a downpour that had seemed inevitable since we left the tee. It didn't put any spectators off though, they remained rooted as the drama continued, Bruce cleaning up for a birdie while Douglas and I lined up our attempts. I was one shot ahead at this stage and harbouring expectations of a two shot lead a few moments hence, I had confidence in Fred's ability to convert my putt, equally I felt Douglas would muff his because nerves would take hold. I was half right, Freddie dutifully drained my putt for me but miraculously, Douglas followed me in with one of those express train efforts which would have careered off the green had the hole not intervened. Not to worry, a slender lead for me to take to the final hole but a lead all the same, and with Freddie at the helm, relentlessly registering birdies, and the now torrential rain making life difficult for Douglas, I was about to cement the victory which would fill my wallet and give me worldwide fame. Not bad for an afternoon's work.

More thunder serenaded our walk to the eighteenth tee and with it a couple of bolts of lightning which was a little disconcerting, lightning freaks people out at the best of times but never more so than on an exposed golf course. Despite this, nobody moved an inch, history was being made, a moment in time that people could tell their grandchildren they'd witnessed.

Douglas was chuntering away, disgusted with the pandemonium going on around him, envious of his playing partner, but suspicious too. Bruce was at ease, as was I, until I looked up and saw a demented Derek flailing his arms around like a windmill, desperately trying to attract my attention. He was standing about a hundred yards away, up on the car park, while I stood on the eighteenth tee waiting for the green to clear. What was up with him? Had the excitement become too much? I beckoned him over since there'd be a few minutes yet before I'd get to tee off. He rushed forward, almost coming a cropper as he ran down the hillside at full tilt until arriving alongside me in a state of blind panic.

Once he caught his breath he blurted out 'you gotta change yer ball, you gotta change yer ball.'

'Calm down Derek... and keep your bleedin' voice down n'all', I told him, 'take a breath and tell me what's up.' The poor chap looked like he was about to have a seizure, I doubted his legs had carried that burly frame of his at such speed for decades and his frantic face suggested he had a ticking time bomb in his underpants.

'Alex, you've got to change your golf ball', he repeated for a third time, 'this climate does all sorts of things with the receiver inside.' He managed to blurt out in between wheezes, 'rain it can cope with, but lightning? Forget it.' With that he placed both hands on his knees to recover from his headlong sprint, leaving me scratching my head.

'We've only had a couple of flashes, nothin' major.'

'That's all it takes Alex. One flash and you're gone, it cuts out the connection between the operating device and the receiver' he muttered in staggered breaths, hands still on knees and head facing the floor. 'Use another ball instead.'

'How do you know it's corrupted for sure?' I whispered, given several hundred people were standing close by and attempting to listen in, fascinated by this unexpected gate crasher. Their suspicions aroused, I tried to play it cool with a demeanour of calm although I was dying a thousand deaths.

'Because I'm the bloody inventor' snapped a recovering Derek, now rising to his full height. 'I trialled this product more times than you've had hot dinners and only one fault was identified, not that you'd call it a fault, there's bugger all I can do about acts of God, but ninety nine per cent of the time a flash of lightning cuts the connection.'

'Ninety nine per cent you say?' my mood momentarily lifting, 'so one per cent of the time it isn't affected at all?' He could see where I was going with this and replied with a great deal of caution.

'The other one per cent was split two ways. Either the connection was restored without fault or it was restored not to the original receiver, but to the nearest electronic receiver to where the previous one had capitulated.'

I pondered his response, the eighteenth green now clearing and my tee shot imminent. I'd owned up to him about my intentions when we'd met earlier in the week and agreed to cut him in if he kept schtum. He'd lose a lot of money if we surrendered now. A smiling Douglas ushered me forward, carrying a smug look, he'd delighted in the panicked exchange between Derek and I, while not knowing the detail of our conversation he surmised that something major was going down.

'On the tee then Russon, can't keep your audience waiting' he announced at the top of his voice, a huge grin spread across his conceited face. I could have smacked him in the chops there and then. The crowd applauded, some shouted encouragement, others cheered, my public awaited in fevered expectation, like the Holte End in the Seventies would suck the football into the back of Villa's opponent's net, the assembled throng here at Stonehaven Golf Club were clamouring to will my golf ball into the hole in no more than two shots. This was intense.

'What'll I do Derek?' I pleaded, leaning forward and pretending to look for something in my golf bag to buy some time. 'I need to know right now, no messing about.'

'Two options. One, play a different ball and hope you're good enough to birdie the hole under your own steam or two, use the same ball and risk setting off some old biddy's pacemaker instead. You could have a death on your hands man!'

Oh the dilemmas of top level sport, trust your own ability or risk illegal performance enhancing products. I knew now how Lance Armstrong had felt, and Eastern European gymnasts, long distance runners, Canadian sprinters, you name it, I was in good company. I looked around and found thousands of excited, expectant faces. These people had dropped everything to witness this moment, these were my people, already I considered them friends, I couldn't possibly let them down. No, there was really no choice to make, I'd risk Derek's ball and if it did set off Aunt Betty's pacemaker or total somebody's iPhone that wasn't my problem, plus, I'd still have an outside chance of a birdie if my deactivated golf ball received a good enough stroke from me to reach the green. My mind was made up.

Derek folded his arms as he watched me tee up, indignant of Portlethen. His theory of probability convinced him that I was about to crash and burn spectacularly, the best that could be hoped for would be a face saving bogey without too much evidence to suggest the previous seventeen holes weren't an enormous con. I shared his concern, left to my own devices this damned golf ball could go anywhere, if only that lightning hadn't struck I'd have been on easy street. Perhaps I'd be lucky and find Derek's previous experiments didn't apply to today's events, that my ball would remain as one with Freddie's directing fingers, his ability on that Kindle shining through as one last time my golf ball sailed through the skies to nestle alongside the flagstick. I looked up at the clubhouse to see if Fred was at the window, and he was, waving enthusiastically, jumping up and down like a cat on a hot tin roof, delirious. He must have done it, achieved the fifty, won the hundred quid! I too had won the jackpot, was a millionaire, if, if, if I could convert the final birdie that he'd seemingly achieved already on my behalf. Fred was oblivious to my skulduggery, so were the thousands around him, except for a simmering Derek who looked on with horror by the side of the tee.

So to the moment of truth, the final tee shot, the unravelling of an imperious round of golf or the consummation of a world record with all the riches and stardom that followed? I selected a four iron, took a gulp, pierced Douglas with a frosty gaze and placed my ball upon the tee peg. Encouragingly, the ball appeared to glint back at me, was that a faint flicker from the epicentre or just wishful thinking? The skies remained pitch black but there'd been no more lightning, perhaps the single flash earlier hadn't been sufficient to upset the connection between Freddie and my ball. In retrospect, it hadn't been a flourishing spike lighting up the skies, more of an apologetic crackle, a humble sparkler rather than a pyrotechnic firework display, surely not enough to violate an innocuous mechanism such as my golf ball?

Verily and forthwith, it came to pass that I did smite the golf ball before me, looking up to the sky in anticipation of its flight toward the green, one hundred and ninety yards ahead. The gathered thousands did likewise, willing my ball skyward and onward to the green, desperate to share with me the wonder of world record breaking, to see Stonehaven put on the map, an eternal new home for the game of golf, replacing St Andrews as the 'Mecca' to which golfing worshippers would flock.

My golf ball did indeed advance skyward, the first half of its journey suggesting a possible entrance to the green, but as it faded feebly to the right towards a destination in the semi rough beneath the practice putting green, it was overtaken in mid air by a huge, white missile with wheels, an unidentifiable flying object if ever there was one. The crowd, and myself, stood with mouths agape as this fridge freezer sized object flew through the air, descended upon the green, created a pitch mark to end all pitch marks, and finished proudly alongside the flagstick. What in the dickens was that?

The crowd fell silent, all eyes turned to me and, appropriately, a deep roll of thunder came from the sky. Now that it was stationary, the flying object was clearly discernible as Keith Douglas's golf trolley, his set of clubs strewn across the fairway having been scattered from the skies during its journey, his juice bottle lying in a greenside bunker and the half eaten pork pie which he'd been devouring, now being removed from the green by the beak of a grateful seagull who thought Christmas had arrived early. In the pantheon of tumbleweed moments, this was up there with the declining of a nationally broadcast marriage proposal.

Presently, the silence was broken by the shouts and yelps of an eight year old boy, excitedly cavorting down the hill from the clubhouse, clasping a shiny black Kindle and shouting 'I did it Dad, I did it! I shot fifty at Stoney, I've won!' before leaping into the arms of his father while the world looked on.

'Fit's he sayin?' chimed Douglas, 'fifty around Stoney?'

'Yeah, Dad said if I could score fifty on my golf app I'd win a hundred pounds, and I've done it, look!'

And with that my own son handed the unequivocal cast

iron evidence of the whole charade directly into the hands of my nemesis, Keith bleedin Douglas. At least Judas delivered his betrayal with a kiss, not Freddie, he handed Douglas my death warrant by hand. Contained on the Kindle now in the bugger's mitts, was a carbon copy, not only of my scorecard, but the precise way my score had been achieved, the app having an instant replay function of every hole completed, an undeniable direct replica, perfect in its every detail.

Douglas instantly called across a member of the committee as witness to the footage (you have to admire his immediate presence of mind when looking to bring a man to book), and the pair of them fast forwarded through the first four holes until deciding they'd seen enough. Bruce asked what was going on, several spectators advanced towards us asking the same question and Derek ran for the hills before his cover could be blown. I mumbled some words suggesting coincidence and misunderstanding but my heart wasn't in it, I'd been tumbled. The committee member dialled for the police but he needn't have bothered, Douglas had already done so, such a fine pillar of the community that man, protecting the public from lawlessness wherever he found it. The tosser.

'I f*ckin kent it Russon, kent it a' along. The only wy you can break eighty is by cheating but this takes the biscuit, kiddin' yer ain loon inta cheatin' fir ye.'

'Mind your bloody language Douglas, there's kids about' I responded with a degree of faux indignance. 'It's all your fault anyhow, you ruined me and I'm reduced to this. How else could I provide for my family?'

'By getting a job?'

'I did, but you paid me buttons, remember?'

'Hire a monkey, you pay peanuts Russon.'

'Come here and say that, I'll give you a bloody good hiding.'

'Come ahead then Russon, I'll brain you, you frickin cheat.'

Ian, the club captain was now in attendance and had heard just about enough, he stepped forward to admonish the pair of us.

'We have enough of a pantomime already gentlemen without your brawling making it worse. Russon, bugger off, I'll have words with you later. Keith, for heavens sake complete your final hole and we'll gather our thoughts afterwards. How in the name of my sainted Aunt I'm going to save the club's reputation after this shambles I do not know.'

'I ken now why Bain the bookie was talkin' aboot some nutter bettin' on hiself winnin' the day, must have been you Russon eh?'

'Maybe it was. I tend to put my money where my mouth is Douglas, I don't waste it on petty court proceedings.'

'Well perhaps you should, didnae dee me ony harm' he snorted, condescending to the last.

Tail between my legs, I shuffled off to the locker room but not before the unmitigated humiliation of having to walk, alone, all the way to the green to fetch Douglas's trolley and return it to him. My 'shot' had knackered his remote control system and the merciless sod had insisted I retrieve his clubs personally.

'Nae takin' a shovel for the pitchmark Russon?' he shouted after I'd walked fifty yards, he was enjoying this.

Talk about a walk of shame, it took an eternity, five thousand pairs of eyes searing their gaze into me, it was crippling, like the walk from the halfway line in a penalty shootout, or clambering up the steps to the gallows. The journey to the green was bad enough, serenaded as I was by catcalls and random abuse, but the return was ten times worse because, by then, word of the tawdry circumstances of Keith's trolley arriving on the green had spread like wildfire. I was booed all the way back to the tee, pelted with fruit, bottles, golf balls and anything else the spectators found launchable. Arriving at the tee, I hurled the trolley at Douglas and exited stage right, pausing only to cough loudly in his backswing in an attempt to put him off. I needn't have bothered, in a final insult he knocked it stone dead, stuck two fingers in my direction and reached for his putter. The b#stard.

The people who'd gathered in the car park also welcomed me with dog's abuse. 'You're a disgrace', 'I'll tear you apart', and 'you f*cking sh#thouse' amongst the kinder remarks.

'Close your ears son' I implored Freddie, 'these people are just a little annoyed with Daddy, it'll be alright.'

'What's a w#nker Daddy' he asked weakly through a veil of tears, 'and why is that policeman pointing at you?'

Blimey, news travelled fast. PC McNee was already on the scene, handcuffs at the ready, shooing me towards the waiting panda car. Be grateful for small mercies I thought, another five minutes and I'd have needed an ambulance not a police car. Brenda, the club's beautiful barmaid and salt of the earth, stepped forward to console Freddie as his father was bundled into custody and as I inched my way slowly past the yelling crowd, baying for my blood, I caught a glimpse of Keith Douglas, arms aloft as he vacated the final green, accepting the club championship trophy as he reached the steps, blowing kisses to the crowd. As bad days at the office go, this one was up there.

CHAPTER THIRTY FOUR

Epitaph

My dearest Harry, Hattie, Emily, Freddie & Ernie

I write to you with a heavy heart, somewhat ashamed that my children must read a letter from their father, written on Her Majesty's Prison's notepaper, nevertheless, we must live with the cards we're dealt. I don't want you to worry, I'm coping well with the 23 hours a day solitary confinement and learning to live with the rigours of prison life. The food is taking some getting used to, who knew that cockroaches could survive in a bowl of porridge? Their saltiness brings a bit of variety to my diet I suppose.

I've not had a visitor since being incarcerated eighteen months ago. Perhaps my friends and family have all suffered prolonged car trouble and it's coincided with the lengthiest bus and train strikes in history? I wouldn't know, all privileges were removed from me the moment I was imprisoned, just my luck that the governor is a Bluenose.

I hear Keith Douglas has married your mother. That's nice. I'm sure she'll be very proud to be betrothed to the very man responsible for your father's twelve year incarceration. His lawsuit during the winter league and subsequent cliping regards my championship betting initiative was uncalled for in my estimations but I'm sure he had his reasons when decimating your father's life forever. Your mother's winning of the national lottery shortly after divorcing me was, I'm sure, a mere coincidence, and not a catalyst for him to start courting her. I hope they live happily ever after and do not meet an untimely demise when I'm released in a decade's time, it'd be awful for them to be walking together alongside Stonehaven's harbour walls and find themselves falling into the sea having been struck by two stray bullets from a distant shotgun.

Enough chit chat from me, I'd better return to breaking rocks and scrubbing lavatories with a toothbrush. Live long and live well, whatever your thoughts of your father, stand tall and know that for one moment in time, in July 1986, he was King for a day having triumphed in the Stonehaven Golf Club Junior Championship. Though the intervening thirty five years may have proved an unmitigated disaster, nothing will ever take that away. Not even Keith bloody Douglas.

With love

Your Dad

A Potted History of Stonehaven Golf Club

1888 – Stonehaven Golf Club is formed, first captain WD Innes. It starts as 10 holes but is reduced to 9 within one year.

1889 – The clubhouse (by Skatie Shore) is officially opened. (The original chimney breast still stands by the 15th tee).

1895 – Club's annual income is £4 (15/- membership fee). Club Secretary (A Wood) is the nephew of the pneumatic tyre inventor (Robert W Thomson)

1897 – New clubhouse is opened. Beer and whisky are 4d.

1904 – Eighteen hole course is opened

1906 – James Braid plays an exhibition match (scores 75, 73)

1909 – Clubhouse is extended

1932 – Sunday play now permitted, provided it commences after 1.30pm

1934 – Field (holes 9-12) now played before the gully (holes 13-15)

1935 – Starters hut erected

1940 – German bomb causes a 30ft x 10ft crater on the first hole

1951 – Membership fee £4

1952 – First Ladies Open

1957 – Sheep stop grazing on the course

1965 – First snooker table

1975 – Estate owner Alexander Innes dies, heirs agree to sell the course to members

1979 – Gully bridge deemed unsafe and is demolished

1986 – Alex Russon wins the Junior Championship :)

1987 – Membership of 475 men, 84 ladies, 151 juniors

1990s – levy imposed to deal with 2nd hole subsidence

2010 – Groundwater Pavilion replaces junior hut

2015 – house behind 10th green removed

2016 – new greenkeeper's shed erected

Other snippets

The 1920 British Open champion (George Duncan) was briefly Stonehaven club pro.

The 1934 Stonehaven champion was one Ronald MacDonald.

The course record is 60 (Euan Kennedy 2004, Neil Irvine 2007, 2008).

Since we're looking at the history of the club, let's take a look at the progress of two junior members from my junior era. While I was taking my first steps as a p*ss artist in 1986, these two had their heads screwed on and progressed to better things.

Andrew Locke

Andrew won the junior championship in 1988 and 1989, following this by reaching the last sixteen in the Scottish Boys Championships, becoming the North East Boys Champion in the same year and The North East Youth Champion (1991).

He was a good footballer too, playing for Scotland Schoolboys, Montrose FC and turning down a contract with Dundee United, reasoning that one injury could draw the curtain on a football career and it was better to pursue his passion for golf. In 1993 he embarked on the Professional Golfers Association (PGA) journey.

Training out of Banchory Golf Club, with occasional study blocks at The Belfry, he qualified in 1997 as a professional golfer and spent four years as Head Assistant Professional at Banchory before joining Inchmarlow Golf Club as teaching professional. He spent ten years there which included the position of district coach for North East Boys who counted amongst their number James Burn, a Scottish Boys Strokeplay champion, Scottish player of the year and Walker Cup player. He coached other internationals too which put him on the Scottish Golf Union's radar in 2011 when they appointed him as their Academy Coach for the North East.

He was on someone else's radar too. Heard of Paul Lawrie? You should have, he was the British Open Champion at Carnoustie in 1999, coached by his lifelong friend Adam Hunter who tragically died from leukemia in 2011. Following his friend's passing, Paul approached Andrew Locke for coaching, imagine that, former Stoney Golf Club junior champion being asked for a lesson by an Open Champion. Andrew accepted and seemed to pass on some reasonable advice given Paul won the Qatar Masters and Johnnie Walker that season, qualifying also for the Ryder Cup team. They continue to work together and Andrew is Senior Instructor at The Paul Lawrie Golf Centre in Aberdeen, coaching beginners through to professionals, internationals and the Scottish Ladies Order Of Merit winner, Shannon McWilliam. And it all started at Stoney.

Bryan Innes

Back in the eighties, Bryan and I played endless amounts of golf together. We were in our mid teens and of equal ability, it's remarkable to say now, our handicaps just sneaking into single figures having started life in the late twenties. Bryan was a useful footballer too but his dedication was to golf and we'd play every available hour God sent unless the weather intervened, although it'd have to be pretty horrific for us not to play. Today, thirty years after our last game together, we shared eighteen holes of golf again, this time not at Stoney but at Royal Aberdeen where Bryan has a membership alongside his honorary one at neighbouring Murcar. I confess that recovery from alcohol was (and remains) a tough gig, I'll now need to draw on that resolve to recover from the abject humiliation of today's events. Times have changed since we last played and no mistake.

Bryan Innes has a handicap of plus two. To the uninitiated, this means he's so good that golf's handicapping system decrees two strokes must be *added* to his total where the vast majority of players have strokes deducted instead. Handicapping is the method used in golf to generate even competition, to enable players of differing abilities to compete on a level playing field. For example, if an ordinary club snooker player was to take on Ronnie O'Sullivan he'd need a hundred point start to make a game of it or if you played Andy Murray at tennis, he'd need to wear a Batman costume and flippers. Similarly, golfers are handicapped to create a fair game. My handicap is ten and I'd never played alongside a golfer off scratch or better before. I'd heard of Bryan's reputation, that he'd become a cracking golfer, but found it hard to believe he was *all that*, I still remembered the diminutive teenager with a drifting slice and barely enough power to clear Stoney's gully. While I appreciated Innes may have come on a little since the old days, I found it hard to accept he was bringing courses like Murcar to their knees.

Any road up, we alighted at Royal Aberdeen on a quiet Thursday morning for our first game in three decades so I could find out for myself. Four hours later I was sat in the clubhouse dining on a sizeable portion of humble pie. The bloke was absolute dynamite.

Physically, Bryan's a world away from the scrawny teenager I knew him to be, indeed he'd arrived directly from the gym where a personal trainer had put him through his paces while I'd been parked up in a McDonalds drive-thru tucking into a grease fest. He looked the part, well dressed, neat, tidy and groomed while I rocked up wearing ill-fitting strides and an unflattering moob smuggler of a t-shirt. I shambled up to the first tee with my laces undone and mobile phone going off, you could spot the quality player from the duffer and we'd not removed a golf club from the bag yet. Once we did, there followed a complete golfing masterclass, Bryan playing the sort of golf that mortals like me only dream of, my only contribution being a procession of hacks, slaps and duffs. He was absolutely solid, barely a mistake made and if he did err at any point it was quickly redeemed with a recovery shot to bring the house back into order.

It was a peculiar feeling playing golf with Bryan again, chastening in one respect but filling me with pride in another. This was my old mucker, a great pal of yesteryear with whom I'd spent entire summers camped out on Stonehaven Golf Course and look what he'd become, a superb golfer and a smashing bloke. Our lives moved in opposite tangents thirty years ago, there aren't many days when I don't rue my descent into alcohol addiction, it was a pleasure to be reunited like this although it acted as a stark reminder of what might have been. I'm not claiming I'd have been anywhere near as proficient a golfer as Bryan, very few people are, but the years of competitive and sociable golf he'd enjoyed while I was relentlessly (and unsuccessfully) seeking solace in the bottom of a glass were undoubtedly years I'd wasted. If I had my time again I'd live life very differently for sure. Our round at Royal Aberdeen ended with him nailing a mid-iron to the 18th and holing out for a par to complete a 71. He'd got off to a shoddy start by his standards otherwise he'd have scored in the sixties. It's a thrill to see someone hit a golf ball how it's meant to be struck, there's a different trajectory altogether, the ball arrows, it doesn't float, it's under control, doesn't drift. I'd like to say I learned a lot but at forty six I reckon my goose is cooked, I could only stand back and admire. A great day, one I'll treasure, if there are any junior members reading please take note. Becoming a boozer isn't big and isn't clever, becoming a top golfer is.

Here's a summary of Bryan's achievements since we last played together, it's quite a list –

1987	Stonehaven GC Junior champion
1992/98	Six time Stonehaven GC champion
1996	Moved to Murcar to test himself against some of the region's top golfers (Keith Hird, John Fraser, Graham McInnes, Ronnie Brechin)
1998	Won Murcar championship for the first time, went on to win it on a further nine occasions
2002	3rd in Scottish Golf Union's scoring averages and 5th in their Order of Merit.
2003/04	Scottish international
2005	semi-finalist British Mid Amateur
2009	Scottish Open strokeplay 3rd place (bronze medal)
2009	Scottish area team championships (gold medal)
2010	Semi-finalist in Scottish match play
2013	Won North East Open (72 hole Scottish Order of Merit event) for a record 3rd time.

Bryan is the only player to have won a clean sweep of scratch events held in the north east of Scotland and his handicap has been as low as +3.3. It's all a long way from finishing mid-table in the Stonehaven junior section monthly Stableford 1984. Top work Bryan, I'm proud to know you and speak for many in that regard.

Stonehaven Golf Club's Junior Section

The junior section has produced a number of talented golfers over the years and continues to provide a super facility to local kids looking to play their golf within a safe, friendly environment.

There are currently forty junior members, including half a dozen girls, and in years past this has been double or even triple this number but the downturn in the popularity of golf in recent years has affected numbers all over the UK. The minimum age is 8 and once juniors reach the 1st of January of the year in which they will become 18, they're then deemed full members. The majority of junior members are in their teens and the club enters the Aberdeen & District Junior Pennant League every year. Our lowest handicapper is currently 5 and the captain enjoys a two year period before handing the baton on, Junior Convenor's can stay as long as they like, the current incumbent is Chris Taylor. Multiple club champion Neil Irvine was the convenor for ten years or more and leads the junior coaching sessions on Sundays during the summer season.

There are many competitions played through the year and recent changes to the rules mean players can have handicaps up to 54. They play off forward tees until 11 years old when they move to the adult tees. Some full members of the club provide their time as volunteer coaches having passed their Level 1 coaching qualification and juniors looking for further coaching, at Level 2 and above, are passed to local professionals or 'roving pro's' may visit Stonehaven to coach them. Some juniors have dual memberships with other courses in the area but largely they remain at Stonehaven once they become full members unless university or work drags them away. There are links with local schools to bring kids into golf, teach them the basics and develop their interest in the sport, hopefully enticing them away from ipads, tablets and tellies, out into the beauty of Stonehaven's coastline.

Many junior members have gone on to become top notch golfers – Bryan Innes, Andrew Locke and David Ross are mentioned elsewhere in this book but add to that Ross Anderson (now PGA pro/coach at Finchley Golf Club), Keifer Brown twice winner of the Spence Trophy (Aberdeen & District champion) and Scott Murray who pursued a golf scholarship in the USA, to name but a few.

Pennant League Members 2016

Stonehaven
Peterhead
McDonald (Ellon)
Banchory
Royal Aberdeen
Inverallochy
Inverurie
Deeside
Murcar
Portlethen
Kemnay
Cruden Bay
Peterculter
Hazelhead
Aboyne

Stonehaven Golf Club's Ladies Section

There are currently sixty lady members, historically there's been over a hundred at any one time, and there are also fifteen social members. The ladies have an active social scene, often organising fundraisers including quiz nights and theme nights.

Ages range from 26 to 83 with the majority somewhere in the middle. Ladies have specified tee times for their competitions, typically Tuesdays and Thursdays with an hour slot on a Saturday between 2-3pm. The Ladies Captain remains in post for two years before stepping down and the committee currently numbers nine with meetings held every month. Friendly matches are played against local clubs, an annual Ladies Open is held at Stonehaven and there's an outing to a different club every year.

Check out the Ladies Championship scroll of honour and you'll see Fiona Lamont's name on there at least ten times, she played off 5, but was usurped by a fourteen time champion by the name of CB Moncrieff who spread her championships across a twenty nine year period between 1939-1968.

I asked the members of Stonehaven Golf Club to pick three words to describe the place, this is what they came up with...

Home, iconic, short, stunning, hilly, friendly, windy, scenic, local, quirky, fun, forgiving, unforgiving, unpredictable, interesting, freaky, changeable, picturesque, spectacular, brilliant, relaxing, brutal, beautiful, unique, frustrating, tricky, panoramic, tough, welcoming, affordable, sloping, sociable, enjoyable, adventurous, exposed, tiring, testing, uneven, difficult, challenging, annoying, breath-taking.

Favourite hole?	*15th, 1st , 7th*
Least Favourite hole?	*6th, 17th, 14th*
Stoney's signature hole?	*15th, 1st, 7th*

What's your favourite golf course?

Panmure, Carnoustie*, Trump*, St Andrews Old Course*, San Lorenzo (Portugal), Kingsbarns*, TPC Sawgrass, The Brabazon, Tecina – La Gomera, Elgin, Crail, Pearl Valley (South Africa), Silloth & Solway, Gleneagles, Santa Maria, El Chapparal (Spain), Nairn, Cruden Bay, Monifieth, Lossiemouth, Drumoig, Oitavas Dunes, Ballater, Boat of Garten, Simola (South Africa), Fossil Trace (Colorado), Rosemount Blairgowrie, Wentworth

*more than 5 votes

A History of Lifeboats In Stonehaven

Half of the proceeds from this book will be given to the RNLI, a charity that saves lives at sea. Karen Smith kindly provides a history of lifeboats in the town...

On February 9th 1854, the Port of Stonehaven gratefully received a lifeboat rowed from Aberdeen and accepted by the chairman Mr Peter Christian. It was generously provided by a member of the Society Of Friends, Miss Lydia A Barclay.

The following year, on March 12th, a new lifeboat the 'St George' was brought with great ceremony to Stonehaven. On February 27th 1874, whilst going to the aid of the barque 'Grace Darking of Blythe', she capsized when making to enter the Port of Aberdeen, foundered on the rocks behind the south harbour and lost the Coxswain and three of the crew. A memorial stands in Cowie Kirkyard, next to Stonehaven Golf Club's eighteenth green, where two of the men are buried.

The 'St George' was immediately replaced by the 'Star', a 33 foot, 10 oared craft which remained in service until 1888, performing 3 service launches and saving 4 lives.

Thereafter she was replaced by the 'Alexander Black' which performed 11 service launches saving 21 lives, the most memorable being the rescue of the crew of a German sailing ship 'Kishlina' (or 'Hiskelina') which foundered in Stonehaven Bay on December 11th 1911.

The 'Alexander Black' was succeeded in 1916 by a rowing and sailing boat named 'Joseph Ridgeway' This craft had 4 service launches with 7 lives saved before being withdrawn from service in 1934 when the station was closed.

There had been three Coxswains during the period –

1888-1908   Andrew Brown

1908-1930   Robert Davidson

1930-1934   William Christie

A D Class lifeboat was stationed at Stonehaven between 1967-1985 when the station was again closed.

In 2013 the RNLI re-opened the lifeboat station and an Atlantic 75 lifeboat is now stationed at Stonehaven and is housed in the same building on the Old Pier as it's predecessors.

Stonehaven Ladies Lifeboat Guild was formed in 1957 and continues fundraising for the RNLI to this day. Known as Stonehaven Fundraising Branch it organises many events every year raising many thousands of pounds.

The Rotary – Stonehaven

Half of the proceeds from this book will go to Stonehaven's Rotary, here's some information on the wonderful work they do.

The Rotary Foundation is Rotary's own charity. Our simple purpose is to do good in the world. Our mission is to advance world understanding, goodwill and peace through the support of education, the improvement of health and the alleviation of poverty. The Rotary Foundation is an international trust whose trustees are Rotarians. In effect, our Foundation is Rotary in action as an international humanitarian and educational charity.

Rotary International is a worldwide organisation with 32,000 clubs in almost every country of the world. We are committed to service for communities throughout the world. Many Rotarians have vocational skills that they use to support humanitarian and educational projects that help to make their communities better places. The Rotary Foundation harnesses the potential of this worldwide organisation by helping clubs to undertake humanitarian and educational work.

Our Foundation has three main areas of activity:

- To eradicate polio: www.endpolio.org

- To deliver sustainable educational and humanitarian projects through grants to Rotary Clubs all over the world. Read about some of the projects run by Rotary Clubs in District 1010: Scotland North. www.rotary-ribi.org/clubs/homepage.php?ClubID=57

- To foster world understanding, goodwill and peace through the Rotary Peace Centres. To find out more about the Peace Centres. www.rotarypeaceproject.com

Foundation grants can also support Scholarships and Vocational Training Teams.

Fifth Hole

Three and One Winter League

Seventh Hole